*Like A Tree Planted
By the Water…*

*Taking Root
As Life Happens*

By Amy L. Boyd

Like A Tree Planted
By the Water…

Taking Root
As Life Happens

By Amy L. Boyd

Like A Tree Planted By the Water: Taking Root As Life Happens

Copyright © 2016 by Amy L. Boyd
ISBN 13: 978-0-692-81530-4
ISBN 10: 0-692-81530-9
Library of Congress Control Number: 2016920595
Amaradia, Carnegie, PENNSYLVANIA
Published by: AmAradia
Printed by CreateSpace
Cover and interior designs: Tamarr's Creative Services
Author Photo: Aaron Jones

Bible Versions and Translations:
AMP: Amplified Bible
CEB: Common English Bible
ESV: English Standard Version
GNT: Good News Translation
GW: God's Word Translation
KJV: King James Version
MSG: The Message
NASB: New American Standard Bible
NIV: New International Version
NLT: New Living Translation
NLV: New Life Version
TLB: The Living Bible
TNIV: Todays' New International Version

For my husband and daughter…
you are the smile on my lips

INTRODUCTION

He will be like a tree that is planted by water.
It will send its roots down to a stream.
It will not be afraid in the heat of summer.
Its leaves will turn green.
It will not be anxious during droughts.
It will not stop producing fruit.
Jeremiah 17: 8 GW

From the writings, to the title, to my fascination with trees, this book wrote itself. The truth is, God took the pen and keyboard and had His way. I began writing these devotionals as a response to what I read during my study time and I share them with you as a source of encouragement. My prayer was, is, and will always be that the words the Lord allows me to write will be a blessing to its readers. I have included the dates at the bottom of some of the entries to show the year of my initial reflection on the topic.

This book chronicles God's faithfulness through life's transitions. "We have no idea what a new year will bring, but God's word will provide the guidance we need." These words will be found within the final devotion of this book. How true they proved to be. They were scribed at the close of 2013 and during the summer of 2014, our father's dementia began to take its toll. We watched a slow decline, slow because daddy was a warrior. He was like a tree planted by the water. God kept our father and our family during the battle, and in 2016, he won the war. Our Heavenly Father called him home to fight no more.

As I contemplated a table of contents, I looked up the parts of a tree. Roots, soil, trunk and crown spoke to my spirit, "No crown without roots…" He's got his crown.

I believe if you commit to prayer before and during your time of devotion to the Lord, the Holy Spirit will lead you on your path through this book. If you choose to read this book in the mornings, it will serve as a great start to your day with the Lord. During your reflection of the day is another time to incorporate the reading of this book into your devotions. God may call you to ask yourself, "How'd I do? How can I do things differently?" and my favorite, "Where would I be without you, Lord?"

Whether you are led to read by page or section, morning, or evening, God promises to meet you there.

Stay rooted…

FOREWORD

In Psalm 1:1-3 (ESV) the Psalmist declares:
"Blessed is the man
who walks not in the counsel of the wicked,
nor stands in the way of sinners,
nor sits in the seat of scoffers;
but his delight is in the law of the Lord,
and on his law he meditates day and night.
He is like a tree planted by streams of water
that yields its fruit in its season,
and its leaf does not wither.
In all that he does, he prospers."

The Psalmist reminds readers that the man that delights in the law of the Lord is blessed! He goes onto describe this man as being like a tree...rooted...planted...by streams of water. The Psalmist paints a beautiful image of what is promised to those that make it a point to root themselves in the Lord and His word.

Fortunately, the very law that the Psalmist speaks of inspires what you hold in your hand; it draws you to the heart of the God that desires to write his law on the hearts of those that draw near to it. Amy Boyd has crafted a work of literature that invites readers to drink from the living water that they may not thirst again. This book is designed for those that desire to be planted in Christ in the midst of a world and culture that threatens to uproot us daily. It will speak to your spirit, challenge your mind and feed your soul. Read it, engage it, discuss it, apply it and let it strengthen you as you learn to take root in Him.

Pastor Brian and Reverend Dionne Edmonds,
Macedonia Church of Pittsburgh

CONTENTS

Section 1
ROOTS

Section 2
SOIL

Section 3
TRUNK

Section 4
CROWN

ROOTS

*the part of the tree that attaches itself
to the soil, holding it steady and
providing nourishment*

Careful Thought

*Now this is what the LORD Almighty says: "**Give careful thought** to your ways.*

*This is what the LORD Almighty says: "**Give careful thought** to your ways.*

*"'Now **give careful thought** to this from this day on—consider how things were before one stone was laid on another in the LORD's temple.*

*'From this day on, from this twenty-fourth day of the ninth month, **give careful thought** to the day when the foundation of the LORD's temple was laid. **Give careful thought:**...*
Haggai 1: 5 7; 2: 15, 18 (NIV)

The book of Haggai is only two chapters long, yet five times, God directs the people to "Give careful thought..."

God is calling us to give careful thought to our actions; both previous and present. Why both? So, we can see what led up to where we are and to see where we are in order to gauge where we need to go.

I believe the Lord wants us to consider two major questions:
1. Is our present way of living productive to the Kingdom?
2. How do we plan to build His house (temple, body of God, Kingdom) from its present state?

Worship: Look

> *¹ I look up to the mountains—*
>   *does my help come from there?*
> *² My help comes from the Lord,*
>   *who made heaven and earth!*
> Psalm 121: 1-2 NLT

"*I look up to the mountains-*" Regardless the version/translation, when looking up to, looking to, or lifting eyes to, one can assume the looker is not in an elevated position or state. One could be in a valley or on flat ground, but not at "the top of the mountain". I love the question, "*...does my help come from there?*" because it's a question of self-encouragement; a reminder; an assurance. If you have ever encouraged yourself, you know the language that must be used. For me, it is not the same as encouraging someone else. I know all the details and background and when I am in a low place, I have to pump myself up. I have to bring to remembrance some of what God has already done in my life.

*Remember when you were depressed, remember when they counted you out, remember when you counted yourself out, remember when there was sickness in your family, remember when you were in debt...*It gives me strength remembering what my God has done and will do.

"*My help comes from the Lord, who made heaven and earth!*" Just in case satan tries to block my memory or cloud my focus, I can look around me and see God's hand in everything. Verse 2 is a statement of His mightiness - Elohim!

Psalm 121 is a song for pilgrims ascending to Jerusalem for Festival; they are going to worship. As I go through the remainder of this week and whatever comes my way, I want my focus to be on where my help comes from. If I meditate on this daily, my heart will be prepared for worship.

Worship: No sleep, no slumber

³ He will not let your foot slip—
  he who watches over you will not slumber;
⁴ indeed, he who watches over Israel
  will neither slumber nor sleep.
Psalm 121: 3-4 (NIV)

"*He will not let your foot slip-*" My foot slipping indicates a
struggle to stay grounded. The struggle can be with someone
or something, but I am already secure in my footing because He
will not allow it to slip. "*…indeed, he who watches over Israel will
neither slumber nor sleep.*" I can trust that God is always watching
over me. I looked up various meanings for slumber and sleep
because the Psalmist made it a point to say "indeed" God "will
neither slumber nor sleep". It's bigger than sleeping and
dozing.

To slumber is to be in a state of inactivity, negligence,
quiescence, or calm and to sleep is to be careless or unalert; to
allow one's alertness, vigilance, or attentiveness to lie dormant.

Hallelujah! There is no inactivity, negligence, carelessness,
inattentiveness or dormancy with God. There are times when
God seems quiet in our lives and we wonder what He is doing.
We can trust that His quietness is neither slumber nor sleep and
whatever He is doing - He is actively doing for our good.

Worship: Time for church

When it's time for church, I often feel that I've been waiting for this time all week!

I have had my own services all week - praise and worship, testimony, prayer, Bible study, confessing and repenting of sins...God allows us to have "church" wherever we are, but there is something about entering into God's House with other believers.

We see faces we have not seen in a week or longer. Don't take it for granted, not everyone who started the week finished it. We hug, and some hugs are tighter than others because some weeks are "tighter" than other weeks. There's strength in fellowship.

We hear/read the "Sick and Shut in" list, those who have passed on or praise reports of recovery and healing...we feel compassion, we feel sympathy, we rejoice...

We hear the music and God's word and we feel redeemed, we feel convicted, we feel loved, we feel blessed, we feel God's Holy Spirit...and we feel like going on.

Waiting

¹Unto thee lift I up mine eyes, O thou that dwellest in the heavens.
²Behold, as the eyes of servants look unto the hand of their masters,
and as the eyes of a maiden unto the hand of her mistress;
*so **our eyes wait upon** the LORD our God,*
***until** that he have mercy upon us.*
Psalm 123: 1-2 (KJV)

"How does a servant wait?"

Anytime God asks me a question, there is something within He wants to call my attention to. So, how does a servant wait?

- A servant waits respectfully -not with an attitude of "you owe me". God is so good, we often forget it is not about us.

- A servant waits <u>without</u> grumbling or complaining. When we complain it is against God. If you believe in the Lord, then you know He is in control of everything. Therefore, your complaints are against Him. Even something as simple as a schedule change at work…Go ahead and grumble, but know who you are really making your complaint against…

- A servant waits with his/her eyes upon the Lord, lest we look away and miss the blessing of God. Keep your focus on God.

- The very nature of a servant is to serve, so serve while you wait on the Lord. Our **eyes wait upon the Lord**, not our limbs. Quit sitting and wondering, get up and get to work for the Lord.

Each point leads to a servant knowing his/her place in relationship to the Master. Don't call yourself a "servant of the Most High", if you are unable to have the countenance of a servant. Servants are humble, respectful, and reverent; not spoiled and lazy.

Our Help: Nine words

If the LORD had not been on our side—
  let Israel say—
² if the LORD had not been on our side
  when people attacked us,
³ they would have swallowed us alive
  when their anger flared against us;
⁴ the flood would have engulfed us,
  the torrent would have swept over us,
⁵ the raging waters
  would have swept us away.
Psalm 124: 1-5 (NIV)

If you know, like I know, those nine words bear repeating! Verse 2 makes it clear that we will be attacked, but with the Lord on our side, we won't be consumed. If at any time during today or this week, you feel overwhelmed, reflect on these words: "swallowed", "engulfed", and "swept over". Each word is a description of what happens when God is **not** on our side. In other words, it can be worse. Your "issue" will remain, but unless you choose to stay in a low state of mind, I guarantee you will shake your head and keep pressing. You might even say, "Thank you!"

Our Help: PTL

6 Praise the Lord, who did not let their teeth tear us apart!
Psalm 124: 6 (NLT)

Praise the Lord (PTL), God is faithful! We have no idea how and from what He is shielding us. When going through a trial, we often feel like we are being ripped or torn apart. We can't imagine how we will recover and we certainly can't imagine it being any worse, but God brings us through. We look back and see we didn't experience the full assault satan had in store for us. Remember, satan's intention is to steal, kill, and destroy us (John 10:10...there is no "or" in this verse, he means to do all three). God is faithful to His word; His plans are not for harm, but for good, prosperity, hope and a future (Jeremiah 29:11).

"If the LORD had not been on our side—" Psalm 124: 1a

Our Help: Stronger

⁷ We have escaped like a bird
  from the fowler's snare;
the snare has been broken,
  and we have escaped.
⁸ Our help is in the name of the LORD,
  the Maker of heaven and earth.
Psalm 124: 7-8 (NIV)

How fragile we would be without trouble? The wind would blow and we would break.

Verse 2 lets us know we would be attacked and now we read in verse 7 that we will be caught in snares (traps). Trials, tribulations and uncomfortable situations are a part of living. Times will get hard, but look to God; the maker of heaven and earth. We get caught in a snare (trap or entanglement), we struggle, and behold - an opening; a way out. Who made the opening; the way out…the Maker of heaven and earth?

"If the LORD had not been on our side——" Psalm 124: 1a

Restoration

[5] Those who sow with tears will reap with songs of joy.
[6] Those who go out weeping, carrying seed to sow, will return with songs of joy, carrying sheaves with them.
Psalm 126: 5-6 (NIV)

Verses 5-6 not only illustrate restoration, but also hope. To sow is to throw or scatter seeds for growth. If I am sowing, I am working with an expectation of growth. The sower is described as working through tears and weeping. The pain and hurt are there, but also present is hope for something better.
2011

Trust

¹THOSE WHO trust in, lean on, and confidently hope in the Lord are like Mount Zion, which cannot be moved but abides and stands fast forever.
Psalm 125: 1 (AMP)

¹⁸ ...the LORD Almighty, who dwells on Mount Zion.
Isaiah 8: 18 (NIV)

I can say I trust God, but what does my trust look like? Is it something seen or only heard about? Trust is more about what we do, than what we say. We have so many little sayings, quotes, and cliches that I sometimes think we are trying to convince ourselves that we do trust God.

The Amplified Version reads, "*trust in, lean on, and confidently hope in the Lord...*" My trust should be visible in the way I live my life. Not only do I need to lean on and hope in Him, but I need to do both CONFIDENTLY.

When was the last time you leaned against something you thought couldn't hold your weight? Did you 'kinda' hope it would, but still brace yourself for the fall, or did you lean because you had confidence in the strength of the structure? No one in their right mind would lean on an unsteady object.

God dwells on Mount Zion, those who put their trust in God are like Mount Zion; so God dwells in those who put their trust in God are united with Him.

Placing your trust in anything or anyone other than the Lord is like leaning against a weak structure. You will fall.

Unless

¹ Unless the LORD builds the house, the builders labor in vain.
Unless the LORD watches over the city, the guards stand
watch in vain.
² In vain you rise early and stay up late,
toiling for food to eat—
for he grants sleep to those he loves.
Psalm 127:1-2 (NIV)

These verses do not discourage labor, standing watch, or toil.
What is discouraged is working in our own strength.

UNLESS the Lord, …we are in vain. To do; perform; act; or carry
out any action without the Lord is to be without effect or avail;
it is of no purpose. Anything we commit our hands to must be
through the Lord, or else it is done in vain.
2011

Standing accused

¹Then he showed me Joshua, the chief priest, standing in front of the Messenger of the Lord. Satan the Accuser was standing at Joshua's right side to accuse him.
Zechariah 3:1 (GW)

Joshua was the high priest and a sinner, like us, who had given satan a position of power in his life. We know this because satan placed himself on the right side of Joshua. The right usually shows dominance or power. Zechariah makes it a point to tell exactly where satan was standing.

When we give a foothold to satan, he becomes very comfortable in our lives and will attempt to keep his position. We, too, get comfortable in our sin and forget that satan, our enemy, stands to accuse us. He wants to expose us in our sin.

The only position satan should have in our lives is UNDER our feet!

¹⁸Jesus said to them, "I watched Satan fall from heaven like lightning. ¹⁹I have given you the authority to trample snakes and scorpions and to destroy the enemy's power. Nothing will hurt you." Luke 10:18-19 (GW)
2011

A burning stick

Praise the Lord!
In verse 1, satan stands to accuse Joshua. Then in verse 2, the Lord rebukes satan; ***twice***. The Lord rebukes him once and then again establishing His relationship to Joshua. Joshua is a sinner, saved by mercy and grace. satan stands close in order to shame us, condemn us, and make us feel guilty, but God steps in! Praise the Lord!

We are "burning sticks snatched from the fire". "***Is not*** *this man a **burning** stick snatched from the fire?*" shows present tense. We are always in need of our Lord to step in and speak for us. Glory to God!

What a loving God we serve. He sees us, standing in our sin, He chooses us. He lets the enemy know that WE ARE HIS. God has empowered us, through Him, to put satan in his proper position - under our feet.

What a beautiful day in the Lord!
2011

Filthy Clothes

³ Now Joshua was dressed in filthy clothes as he stood before the angel. ⁴ The angel said to those who were standing before him, "Take off his filthy clothes."

Then he said to Joshua, "See, I have taken away your sin, and I will put fine garments on you."
Zechariah 3: 3-4 (NIV)

Who removed the filthy clothes? It wasn't Joshua.
These verses make it clear that we are neither equipped to remove our sin, nor are we expected to. Stop trying in your own strength. Like Joshua, we come before the Lord in our filthy garments of sin, and **God** cleanses us. Not only does He take away our sin; He makes us new. Hallelujah!
2011

Clean turban

Then I said, "They should also place a clean turban on his head." So they put a clean priestly turban on his head and dressed him in new clothes while the angel of the Lord stood by.
Zechariah 3: 5 (NLT)

Joshua was a high priest who stood accused before the Lord. Though he was a sinner, through the love of God, his priesthood was restored. His filthy garments (sins) were removed and he was made new; justified. The turban was part of the priestly garments, but it was more distinctive. The wearing of turbans was a sign of royalty.

I believe the significance of the turban is two-fold. I believe it was to set him apart as royalty, but also for the renewing of his mind. God saves us, restores us and sets us apart, but if our mind is not renewed…satan can come in and convince us that we are NOT new creatures. satan will make us think that God has "fine print" forgiveness. It should hurt our hearts when we sin. We are convicted and repent, but sometimes we don't forgive ourselves. God has cast it away. He will never bring it up again, but with the help of the enemy, we revisit what is dead and gone. We will never live the full life God has for us, if we don't accept His unconditional love. We are new creatures - Hallelujah!
2011

My mouth

A person with good sense is patient, and it is to his credit that
he overlooks an offense.
Proverbs 19: 11 (GW)

When I was in my early twenties, my father would frequently
ask, "Do you always have to have something to say?" He was
referring to my ability to argue any and everything; big or
small. The truth is, at that point in my life, I did always have
something to say. You wouldn't have said it to me, if you didn't
want me to respond. I felt it my duty to set the record straight.
Obviously, I did not have good sense.

Somewhere along the line, I found life to be much more
peaceful when I learned to breathe and consider words before
speaking them. I began to consider the source, the
consequences of my reply and the importance/validity of the
words spoken to me. I learned that sometimes people do mean
their words for harm and sometimes they don't. Sometimes
people are having a bad day, sometimes responding is not worth
it, and sometimes the truth hurts…

At times, I still struggle with keeping the doors to my mouth
shut, especially when offended. I praise God for stepping in! I
give God all the glory because I know, left to my own devices, I
will speak and look foolish. I will discredit myself, but more
importantly my response or my responding could dim my light
in already dark places. Life is about so much more than my hurt
feelings or my having a response.
2011

Plow for it

Those too lazy to plow in the right season will have no food at the harvest.
Proverbs 20: 4 (NLT)

Plowing is the hard work; requiring action and sweat. It's the digging, cutting into, turning over and pushing through.
It is: saying no to extra dessert or french fries and yes to exercise; working the extra hours to pay off debt; saying yes to studying on a warm sunny day; saying no to the upgrades you are eligible for; disciplining when you don't feel like it; saying yes to getting up a little earlier to hear from the Lord, etc...

This may apply to you in some way, but I am talking to myself right now. I have found myself mentally and verbally complaining about a blessing that is going to require some extra work from me. I enjoy when God lays the blessings out and I pick them up and rejoice. There are times God blesses and says, "Plow for it!"

If you want to be healthy. "Plow for it!"
If you want to save money, stop spending needlessly. "Plow for it!"
If you want a disciplined child, discipline yourself and provide structure. "Plow for it!"
If you want a relationship with the One who created you; get up, study, talk, and listen. "Plow for it!"

Lord, please forgive me for my complaining, ungrateful, and lazy spirit. Thank you for loving me enough to show me. Please renew my mind, create in me a clean heart and a right spirit! Give me strength to Plow for it! In the name of Jesus, Amen.

2011

Wait

²⁹The wicked bluff their way through, but the virtuous think before they act."
Proverbs 21: 29 (NLT)

We live in a world that moves fast. We don't have to wait to eat, we don't have to wait to respond or get a response, and we don't have to wait for information. Most things are at our finger tips, yet there is something to be said for taking our time and waiting.

In order to be virtuous or upright, we must be willing to slow down and wait for God. Thinking before we act requires that we consult God first. We often want to rush and act before God has revealed all we need to know. This is evidence of our need to be in control; our lack of submission. Reflect on the outcomes of your rushing...When I think of the decisions I have made on my own, I thank God for reminders like today's verse.

Set apart

⁵A devious person has thorns and traps ahead of him. Whoever guards himself will stay far away from them.
Proverbs 22: 5 (GW)

To guard myself is to set myself apart. Yes, the Lord has set us apart, but we must also take action to do the same. We must guard ourselves from things, people, and places that are in opposition to God. Being in opposition to God is not only the obvious, but also the "seemingly" small things that give satan a foothold to lead us to a path of thorns and traps.

The content of what we watch, listen to, or talk about feed our spirits; our souls. What are we feeding our souls? Is it nourishing our soul or our flesh? Is it building us up or breaking us down? Like it or not, some things have to go for us to grow. Prudence, humility, fear of the Lord, righteousness, and self-discipline are how we guard ourselves; our souls.
2011

Lion and the lamb

Revelation 5: 5-7 (NIV)
⁵ Then one of the elders said to me, "Do not weep! See, the Lion of the tribe of Judah, the Root of David, has triumphed. He is able to open the scroll and its seven seals."
⁶ Then I saw a Lamb, looking as if it had been slain, standing at the center of the throne, encircled by the four living creatures and the elders. The Lamb had seven horns and seven eyes, which are the seven spirits of God sent out into all the earth. ⁷ He went and took the scroll from the right hand of him who sat on the throne.

Lion of Judah **and** Lamb of God!

Part 1:

God is love! Only love can provide a lion and a lamb. Both speak to the very nature of God. The Lion is strong enough to protect us and tear to pieces anything coming against us, yet the lamb is gentle enough to die for our sins. satan thought he conquered Jesus Christ through crucifixion, but God defeated him with the resurrection and ascension.

Part 2:

Fathers pass on traits to their children and our Heavenly Father is no exception. He enables us to stand as a lion or a lamb, whichever brings **Him** the glory. I have a friend who has been harassed by her supervisor. After a final encounter, she clearly heard God tell her to stand and fight. She requested a meeting with her tormentor, had a mediator, and brought forth her case. She had gathered enough information to place herself in a position to legally do this person harm. She was humble and respectful, and shared only the facts. God touched the tormentor in such a way that he admitted his wrongdoing and apologized. She accepted the apology and the meeting was over. She, through our Lord, stood like a lion but was gentle as a lamb. She was relieved the ordeal was over, but her joy was because of God blessing her to show mercy. The mediator said she'd never seen a more generous person and had never seen the other person humble. My friend, our sister, came away praising God and giving Him the glory!

She ministered first to her accuser, her mediator, then me, and now I share her story with you as a reminder that we are called to be "doers of the word".

Relationship with God

For this reason, ever since I heard about your faith in the Lord Jesus and your love for all God's people, I have not stopped giving thanks for you, remembering you in my prayers. I keep asking that the God of our Lord Jesus Christ, the glorious Father, may give you the Spirit of wisdom and revelation, so that you may know him better. I pray that the eyes of your heart may be enlightened in order that you may know the hope to which he has called you, the riches of his glorious inheritance in his holy people, and his incomparably great power for us who believe.
Ephesians 1: 15-19a (NIV)

Give thanks and pray for one another. We don't know all of our Christian brothers and sisters, but we know we are related through our inheritance from our Father. Paul was very specific in his prayer for the Ephesians. His prayer was basically that they would become intimate with God and His power.

He prayed that God would give them a Spirit of wisdom and revelation to know Him better.
He prayed for their enlightenment to grasp:
- the hope of His calling;
- the fullness of their inheritance;
- the incomparable great power for them through the Lord

We can pray for one another in the same way.

Moving forward

⁷ I became a servant of this gospel by the gift of God's grace given me through the working of his power.
⁷ By God's grace and mighty power, I have been given the privilege of serving him by spreading this Good News.
Ephesians 3: 7 (NIV), (NLT)

God has been speaking to me about the privilege of serving Him. When is the last time you thought about how your service impacts the Kingdom of God? Not what "you" do, but what God does through you; what He allows you to do...It is humbling.

Since grace is unmerited favor, serving God is something we do not, on our own, deserve to do. Paul was very aware of this grace, yet never dwelled on his past sins. He allowed it (mercy and grace) to fuel his present work and the future blessings it would bring. If we move away from allowing our past to confine us (that is the enemy's desire) and allow it to remind us how marvelous God's grace is, we will be mindful of the ramifications of serving from any place other than one of humility. God's Kingdom doesn't necessarily suffer, but the kingdom within us does.
2011

Careful: This may sting

30 And do not grieve the Holy Spirit of God, with whom you
were sealed for the day of redemption. (NIV)
30And do not grieve the Holy Spirit of God [do not offend or
vex or sadden Him], by Whom you were sealed (marked,
branded as God's own, secured) for the day of redemption (of
final deliverance through Christ from evil and the consequences
of sin).
Ephesians 4:30 (AMP)

My first thought was - How would one grieve the Holy Spirit of
God? Isn't the Holy Spirit a comforter? Perhaps I would grieve
the Spirit by not allowing myself to be comforted…Why would
I not want to be comforted? I guess I don't have to worry about
this verse because I always want the Lord's comfort. God's
word always has application in our lives even when we try
really, really hard NOT to see it. So, how do I grieve the Holy
Spirit?

Verse 30 is the meat wedged in a hearty sandwich! Verses 29
and 31 let us know how we grieve the Holy Spirit. The
Amplified version breaks it down nicely for those of us who
need it broken down. Careful: this may sting.

*29Let no foul or polluting language, nor evil word nor unwholesome or
worthless talk [ever] come out of your mouth, but only such [speech] as
is good and beneficial to the spiritual progress of others, as is fitting to
the need and the occasion, that it may be a blessing and give grace
(God's favor) to those who hear it.*
*31Let all bitterness and indignation and wrath (passion, rage, bad
temper) and resentment (anger, animosity) and quarreling (brawling,
clamor, contention) and slander (evil-speaking, abusive or blasphemous*

language) be banished from you, with all malice (spite, ill will, or baseness of any kind).

I can only speak for myself when I say it stings, badly. I grieved the Holy Spirit on more than one occasion last week. How could our Comforter not be grieved/saddened by such ugliness? We say, do, and think things that He has come to deliver us from. If we allow God to dwell in us and the Holy Spirit to comfort us, we will be strengthened to have the mind of Christ (1 Corinthians 2:16).
2011

Set apart

*⁸ For you were once darkness, but now **you are light in the Lord. Live as children of light…***
Ephesians 5: 8, 11-13 (NIV)

*¹¹ Have nothing to do with the fruitless **deeds** of darkness, but rather expose them. ¹² It is shameful even to mention what the disobedient do in secret. ¹³ But everything **exposed by the light** becomes visible—and everything that is illuminated becomes a light.*

Paul isn't telling the Ephesians to run from evil, he is telling them to have nothing to do with evil deeds. There is a difference. I can work in an environment full of gossip, but I must avoid, abstain, and reject/have nothing to do with it. I need to be light in the darkness.

"but rather expose them." was of interest to me because I began to wonder if I was being called to correct every wrong-doer and/or tell on them. We are not called to expose with our mouths, but with our conduct; our light. People get much more out of what we do than what we say. That's not to say that we don't correct someone verbally, but we have to be careful. Proverbs 14:9 warns us that fools mock at making amends for sin. You can talk to a fool until you are blue in the face and they may provoke you. If you are not alert, you'll make a fool out of yourself. Removing yourself from a situation doesn't require a conversation or an announcement, just get up and go. Someone is watching and will follow.

John 3: 20 and James 4: 7 show us we don't have to run from evil because when we allow our light to shine, evil flees from

our presence. This can explain the attraction some have to you and the aversion others have…
2011

An attack

And let us not lose heart and grow weary and faint in acting nobly and doing right, for in due time and at the appointed season we shall reap, **if we do not loosen and relax our courage and faint.**
Galatians 6: 9 (AMP)

Then you will experience God's peace, which exceeds anything we can understand. **His peace will guard your hearts and minds** *as you live in Christ Jesus.*
Philippians 4:7 (NLT)

Devote yourselves to prayer with an **alert mind and a thankful heart.**
Colossians 4: 2 (NLT)

Yesterday afternoon I became extremely agitated. First I was tired, then hungry, and next discouraged. "Fruitless" and "Why try?" were the words the enemy used. Without going into detail, it was nothing short of an attack. I felt an indescribable heaviness. I praise God for sending me straight to His word! First, I went to the valley of dry bones. Based on the attack, in my mind, everything was dead. Then, the Holy Spirit said, "You can't stop trying." Those words led me to Galatians 6:9. Although the enemy kept questioning it, I kept saying it and thinking it and before I knew it - it was over. (Yes, I prayed but I had to speak God's word aloud.)

I prayed about the experience and meditated on what I needed to do. I thought it was a sneak attack, but God showed me it had been brewing from the time I stepped in the door at work. There were three occurrences - one I experienced, one I heard for myself, and the other was information shared with me. All three agitated me and confirmed why I shouldn't be there. God showed me I was not where I was supposed to be (location). I had made a decision to stay back from where I originally scheduled myself in order to work on another project. In my mind, it was time better spent because I never seem to be productive in that other place…

God showed me to be more prayerful with an **alert** mind and a thankful heart. He showed me when I take it all to Him, I'll have peace - even in dark places. Lastly, He showed me to stop making decisions based on what I feel and what is most comfortable to me.

2011

Praise report

23 Search me, O God, and know my heart;
test me and know my anxious thoughts.
24 Point out anything in me that offends you,
and lead me along the path of everlasting life.
Psalm 139: 23-24 (NLT)

God will show us our offensive ways. He is gracious and wants us to change. His revelation is never for condemnation, but to better us for His glory.

The Lord showed me that I have some "Jonah - tendencies". I have often dwelled on Jonah's running as disobedience. I have prided myself on not running from where God has sent me, but God showed me I, at times, have a poor attitude. I thought because I went where He told me to go that I was doing well. I tend to become frustrated and tired when i don't see growth where i've been planting. In steps, Jonah…I start devising ways to avoid my assignment and working in my own strength (He needs my help…). Disobedience is disobedience, whether we run away aggressively like Jonah or do trot like I've been doing.

God showed me I will not always see growth in the places I've been sent to. My faith and trust in Him must fuel my work. Wanting to see the "fruits of our labor" is a very telling statement of who we are working for…self or God? I forgot it wasn't about me. This may not sound like a praise report because it was a thump on the head, but God is good. I'd rather have a thump on the head than be in the belly of a whale!
2011

Drawing close

⁷ So humble yourselves before God. Resist the devil, and he will flee from you. ⁸ Come close to God, and God will come close to you. Wash your hands, you sinners; purify your hearts, for your loyalty is divided between God and the world. ⁹ Let there be tears for what you have done. Let there be sorrow and deep grief. Let there be sadness instead of laughter, and gloom instead of joy. ¹⁰ Humble yourselves before the Lord, and he will lift you up in honor.
James 4: 7-10 (NLT)

One of my favorite verses is James 4:8. It gives me a sense of comfort knowing that when I come close to God, He is faithful to come close to me. It strengthens me especially when I am seeking Him through prayer and fasting. It is a blessing to share with others as one of God's promises. We do have to be careful that our favorite verses and scriptures do not become "routine" words we speak with our mouths and not know in our hearts.

God led me to place verse 8 back in context in my heart and mind by meditating on verses 7-10.
Humble/submit yourself before God.
Resist evil and it will flee. (now…)
Draw close to God and He will draw close to you. (Don't stop there…)
Lament for **and** repent of your sins. (We get so busy getting forgiveness that we forget to truly be sorry. We don't have to dwell in it, but at least take time to think how we have grieved our Father who art in Heaven.) Humble yourself and God will lift you up! Keep God's word in context in your heart, mind, and mouth.
2011

SOIL

essential in that it allows for healthy growth, not just for the tree itself but for the living organisms around it

The danger of not knowing the power of God

> ⁵ When all the Israelites saw the Ark of the Covenant of the
> Lord coming into the camp, their shout of joy was so loud it
> made the ground shake!⁶ "What's going on?" the Philistines
> asked. "What's all the shouting about in the Hebrew camp?"
> When they were told it was because the Ark of the Lord had
> arrived, ⁷ they panicked. "The gods have come into their
> camp!" they cried. "This is a disaster! We have never had to
> face anything like this before! ⁸ Help! Who can save us from
> these mighty gods of Israel? They are the same gods who
> destroyed the Egyptians with plagues when Israel was in the
> wilderness.
> 1 Samuel 4: 5-8 (NLT)

My initial thought when reading this was, "Look at how Israel
praised and how the enemy shook with fear!" Then I read
further…in verses 9-11, the Philistines "man up" and defeat the
Israelites. Not only do they defeat them, they capture the Ark
of the Lord's covenant. I was disappointed and wondered what
happened…

The enemy knows God's power and is terrified UNTIL he sees
that we don't. The Israelites lost touch with their Power
Source. They thought it was the ark (verse 3)! Don't get
caught up in the representations of God. Our Bibles can't save
us and neither can the words on the pages, IF we don't apply
them to our hearts, minds, and lives. We must live the Word
out. The Israelites praised and shook the ground, but it was
empty. They cheered and rallied for the "entrance" of the ark,
not the power of the Lord that is ever-present! Am I praising
God based on what I want/need or because of who He is and
always will be?

Tap into the power of God

> ⁵ When all the Israelites saw the Ark of the Covenant of the Lord coming into the camp, their shout of joy was so loud it made the ground shake! ⁶ "What's going on?" the Philistines asked. "What's all the shouting about in the Hebrew camp?" When they were told it was because the Ark of the Lord had arrived, ⁷ they panicked. "The gods have come into their camp!" they cried. "This is a disaster! We have never had to face anything like this before! ⁸ Help! Who can save us from these mighty gods of Israel? They are the same gods who destroyed the Egyptians with plagues when Israel was in the wilderness.
>
> 1 Samuel 4: 5-8 (NLT)

The Israelites not only failed to tap into the power of God because they praised the representation and not Him, but God had become an "after-thought" to them.

> ³ **After** the battle was over, the troops retreated to their camp, and the elders of Israel asked, "Why did the Lord allow us to be defeated by the Philistines?" Then they said, "Let's bring the Ark of the Covenant of the Lord from Shiloh. If we carry **it** into battle with us, **it** will save us from our enemies."

Yes, "After..." the battle was over, they thought to go get the ark from Shiloh. (Not on their way or in the midst of battle, but AFTER.) What were they doing before the battle? What were they doing in preparation for the battle? The first verse in chapter 4 reads that Israel went out to fight against the Philistines, so they were not ambushed or caught off guard. I have come to the conclusion that they had become self-reliant and neither God, nor His will were a priority. This is how He becomes a thing in our lives, instead of our Center.

When God has His proper place, we don't ever have to go get Him; He is ever-present. God is not an appliance that we put away until we need/want Him - a vacuum in the closet we pull out to clean up or straighten up a mess. Relationship with God is constant and consistent, regardless of the circumstances. There's ongoing communication (speaking **and** listening). We are reminded to praise God and not the representations of Him. He is not an after-thought.
2011

Turn back to the power of God

⁵ When all the Israelites saw the Ark of the Covenant of the Lord coming into the camp, their shout of joy was so loud it made the ground shake! ⁶ "What's going on?" the Philistines asked. "What's all the shouting about in the Hebrew camp?" When they were told it was because the Ark of the Lord had arrived, ⁷ they panicked. "The gods have come into their camp!" they cried. "This is a disaster! We have never had to face anything like this before! ⁸ Help! Who can save us from these mighty gods of Israel? They are the same gods who destroyed the Egyptians with plagues when Israel was in the wilderness. ⁹ Fight as never before, Philistines! If you don't, we will become the Hebrews' slaves just as they have been ours! Stand up like men and fight!" ¹⁰ So the Philistines fought desperately, and Israel was defeated again. The slaughter was great; 30,000 Israelite soldiers died that day. The survivors turned and fled to their tents. ¹¹ The Ark of God was captured, and Hophni and Phinehas, the two sons of Eli, were killed.
1 Samuel 4: 5-11 (NLT)

The enemy is frightened by the power of God, but the Israelites were unable to tap into that power because they had turned from Him. Their turning away from the Lord is not specifically stated in chapters 1-4, but we know they praised "things" instead of God and that God had become an "after-thought". Confirmation comes in 1 Samuel 7: 2b, "Then all the people of Israel **turned back** to the LORD." You can't turn back if you haven't turned away.

So, how did it get to that point?

(1 Samuel 2: 12, 17, 29)

*¹² Eli's sons were scoundrels; they had **no regard for the LORD**.*

¹⁷ This sin of the young men was very great in the LORD's sight, for **they were treating the LORD's offering with contempt***.*

²⁹ Why do you **scorn my sacrifice and offering** *that I prescribed for my dwelling? Why do you* **honor your sons more than me** *by fattening yourselves on the choice parts of every offering made by my people Israel?'*

When something stinks, it usually starts at the head. Eli was the Judge-Priest of the Israelites, but failed to deal with the wickedness of **his** sons, Hophni and Phinehas, who were also priests. It was known by all, including him, that they were abusing their power. He confronted them, they ignored him, and nothing changed.

The final reason the Israelites could not be blessed by the power of God is because the leadership's contempt for God defiled them. To lead means to go before or with to show the way and that is exactly what they did. They led the people to unrighteousness. Great responsibility comes with being a leader, whether at home, on the job or in ministry! We may say, "What I do is my business…", but people are watching and following, and we may be leading the way to hell.

In order to receive and experience the power of God that makes our enemies shake with fear, we must:
praise God and not representations of Him,
place God at the head of our lives,
and leaders must lead righteously for the sake of their people.
2011

Fear: Man or God?

> *15 Samuel stayed in bed until morning, then got up and opened the doors of the Tabernacle as usual. He was afraid to tell Eli what the Lord had said to him. 16 But Eli called out to him, "Samuel, my son.' "Here I am," Samuel replied.*
> *17 "What did the Lord say to you? Tell me everything. And may God strike you and even kill you if you hide anything from me!"18 So Samuel told Eli everything; he didn't hold anything back. "It is the Lord's will," Eli replied. "Let him do what he thinks best."*
> *1 Samuel 3: 15-18 (NLT)*

Samuel had a lot on his plate! He had the joy of a new level in his relationship with the Lord AND he had to deliver bad news to Eli. Eli was an important part of his life. He had spoken blessings to Samuel's mother while she was praying to have a child. Samuel spent the majority of his life with him, and Eli was the one who revealed who was calling him and how to answer the call. We can understand Samuel's fear. How do you tell the person who has mentored you their time is coming to an end?

He was afraid, but when Eli told him the Lord would deal with him severely for not sharing the entire vision, he had to make a decision about his fear...
Will I fear man or God?

Like Samuel, we often find ourselves with the same question before us. We all have fear, but God does not want us to live and dwell in it. Fear opens the door to all types of demonic influences: doubt, self-reliance, disobedience, and rebellion to name a few.

Samuel chose wisely.   Will we?

> *"For God has not given us a **spirit** of **fear** and timidity, but*
> *of power, love, and self-discipline."*
> *2 Timothy 1: 7 (NLT)*

Irrational Fear

*¹ Now the Lord said to Samuel, "You have mourned long
enough for Saul. I have rejected him as king of Israel, so fill
your flask with olive oil and go to Bethlehem. Find a man
named Jesse who lives there, for I have selected one of his sons
to be my king."² But Samuel asked,* **"How can I do that?
If Saul hears about it, he will kill me."** *"Take a heifer
with you," the Lord replied, "and say that you have come to
make a sacrifice to the Lord. ³ Invite Jesse to the sacrifice, and I
will show you which of his sons to anoint for me."⁴ So Samuel
did as the Lord instructed...*
1 Samuel 16: 1-4a (NLT)

Who will you fear - man or God?
Fear causes us to be irrational when God gives us an assignment
we are uncomfortable with. Saul was unrighteous, yet Samuel
mourned him and was holding on to the past he knew. The
Lord tells him to go anoint the new king and he tells God that IF
Saul hears about it, he will kill him. God was talking to
Samuel...Who was going to tell Saul?
When God tells me to do something or go somewhere I don't
want to, I explain all the reasons I should not. I make sure God
understands all the dangers of me doing or going because I
know He loves me and He wouldn't want any danger to befall
me. Imagine that...me, making sure God has thought it
through. How irrational is it to know or say we know how
much God loves us and then question our safety when told to
move?

Once again, Samuel chose wisely. Will we follow through with
our next difficult assignment or will we cling to what is familiar
and comfortable?

*"For God has not given us a **spirit** of **fear** and timidity, but of power, love, and self-discipline."*
2 Timothy 1: 7 (NLT)

Fear: Wait on the Lord

*Meanwhile, Saul stayed at Gilgal, and his men were trembling
with fear.⁸ Saul waited there seven days for Samuel, as Samuel
had instructed him earlier, but Samuel still didn't come. Saul
realized that his troops were rapidly slipping away. ⁹ So he
demanded, "Bring me the burnt offering and the peace
offerings!" And Saul sacrificed the burnt offering* **himself***.*
*¹⁰ Just as Saul was finishing with the burnt offering, Samuel
arrived. Saul went out to meet and welcome him, ¹¹ but Samuel
said, "What is this you have done?' Saul replied, "I saw my
men scattering from me, and you didn't arrive when you said
you would, and the Philistines are at Micmash ready for
battle. ¹² So I said, 'The Philistines are ready to march against
us at Gilgal, and I haven't even asked for the Lord's help!' So
I felt compelled to offer the burnt offering myself before you
came."¹³ "How foolish!" Samuel exclaimed.* **"You have not
kept the command the Lord your God gave you.
Had you kept it, the Lord would have established
your kingdom over Israel forever.** *¹⁴ But now your
kingdom must end, for the Lord has sought out a man after his
own heart. The Lord has already appointed him to be the
leader of his people, because you have not kept the Lord's
command."*
1 Samuel 13: 7-14

Saul's men were not the only ones afraid. Saul was the king and
his men were trembling with fear, yet we don't read anywhere
that he encouraged them or rallied them with an inspiring
speech. Instead, we read that he was waiting while his troops
were deserting him. We don't read where he set a "warrior"
example.

What was on the king's mind?

His men were trembling with fear.

The man of God hadn't shown up at the time he expected.

His men were deserting him and the Philistines were ready for battle.

Saul was scared and his fear caused him to act on his own. He had no business sacrificing the burnt offering himself, but he did. As soon as he finished the offering, Samuel arrived and questioned his actions. Look at how Saul explains his actions in verse 12. He operated out of fear and disobeyed the Lord. Fear causes us to act apart from God and end up missing our blessing. Once again, we see how we are unable to tap into the power of God when we don't put Him first.

Saul chose to fear men instead of God. What will we do the next time we are surrounded by fear, we feel deserted, and God hasn't shown up when we want? Will we act out of fear or wait on the Lord?

Fasting

²⁵ At the end of forty days they returned from exploring the land.
²⁶ They came back to Moses and Aaron and the whole Israelite community at Kadesh in the Desert of Paran. There they reported to them and to the whole assembly and showed them the fruit of the land. ²⁷ They gave Moses this account: "We went into the land to which you sent us, and it does flow with milk and honey! Here is its fruit. ²⁸ But the people who live there are powerful, and the cities are fortified and very large. We even saw descendants of Anak there. ²⁹ The Amalekites live in the Negev; the Hittites, Jebusites and Amorites live in the hill country; and the Canaanites live near the sea and along the Jordan."³⁰ Then Caleb silenced the people before Moses and said, "We should go up and take possession of the land, for we can certainly do it."³¹ But the men who had gone up with him said, "We can't attack those people; they are stronger than we are." ³² And they spread among the Israelites a bad report about the land they had explored. They said, "The land we explored devours those living in it. All the people we saw there are of great size. ³³ We saw the Nephilim there (the descendants of Anak come from the Nephilim).
Numbers 13: 25-33 (NIV)

We seemed like grasshoppers in our own eyes, and we looked the same to them."
Verse 25 caused me to think of those who may be in a season of fasting, perhaps for 40-days. Forty days never seemed like a long time until I spent it fasting. It is time enough for a journey or an exploration. If you have been led to fast for 40 days, God has led you for a purpose. I believe a purpose of action is intended to follow.

The men sent to scout out the land of Canaan had a purpose. It was to **courageously** (verse 20 KJV) find out what the land was like and return with a report. It was already promised to them by God; they only needed details. The results…The majority became intimidated (fearful) by what their human eyes saw. They forgot the promise and missed the blessing for themselves and delayed it for their offspring.

So, at the end of your journey/exploration/fast, what will you **do**? God is calling you to a new thing!

Will you boldly take hold of your promise or will you see yourself as a grasshopper?

Go boldly

*¹⁶ For **forty days**, every morning and evening, the Philistine champion strutted in front of the Israelite army.³² "Don't worry about this Philistine," David told Saul. "I'll go fight him!"*
³³ "Don't be ridiculous!" Saul replied. "There's no way you can fight this Philistine and possibly win! You're only a boy, and he's been a man of war since his youth."³⁴ But David persisted. "I have been taking care of my father's sheep and goats," he said. "When a lion or a bear comes to steal a lamb from the flock, ³⁵ I go after it with a club and rescue the lamb from its mouth. If the animal turns on me, I catch it by the jaw and club it to death. ³⁶ I have done this to both lions and bears, and I'll do it to this pagan Philistine, too, for he has defied the armies of the living God! ³⁷ The Lord who rescued me from the claws of the lion and the bear will rescue me from this Philistine!"Saul finally consented. "All right, go ahead," he said. "And may the Lord be with you!"
1 Samuel 17: 16, 32-37 (NLT)

Every morning and evening for forty days, Goliath taunted the Israelite armies. Saul and his men were terrified (verse 11) and waiting for "someone" to stand up to this giant. They were waiting for action from some where.

It's a beautiful thing when we realize we are right where God wants us to be. It's a blessing when we can look back over our lives and identify the very things that prepared us for and brought us to our purpose. David found himself in that place while talking to Saul. David knew he was called for this time with Goliath. Everyone else was dismayed and terrified, but David saw the taunts for what they were and was able to put the situation in perspective. The taunts were not personal (we don't fight against flesh and blood), they were against our Lord. Therefore, David knew God would deliver him from the hand of Goliath (if God is for us, who can be against us…).

The battles God has brought us through; the bumps, bruises, and scars prepared us for this present time. God has already equipped us with the weapons and armor we need. Go boldly in the name of the Lord Almighty!

Communities: Take a stand

48 As Goliath moved closer to attack, David quickly ran out to meet him. 49 Reaching into his shepherd's bag and taking out a stone, he hurled it with his sling and hit the Philistine in the forehead. The stone sank in, and Goliath stumbled and fell face down on the ground.
1 Samuel 17: 48-49 (NLT)

I love the fact that David was in battle and behaved like a warrior. He didn't wait around for Goliath to move closer, he ran to meet him and used his weapons. As Christians, we are always under attack, so why do we wait until the enemy gets right upon us to act? David illustrates that we should be prepared and ready to meet the attacks. David was moving in the name of the Lord Almighty. In other words, we should always have our armor on, always be in prayer, and always be prepared so that when we sense the enemy is trying to move in closer - we can go, in the name of Jesus, and knock him to the ground!

The enemy is on the prowl! Watch the news and see that the enemy is after our youth! Listen to the reports and notice where and who is being affected by violence. Are we going to watch, listen, and shake our heads OR are we, as a mighty army of the Living God, going to *run quickly to meet* the enemy? If you haven't begun already, please begin lifting our communities up in prayer. We need a "fresh wind"! Pray for healing in our communities and protection for our youth. Rebuke satan and his tactics of violence, murder, lack, oppression, abuse, apathy, and self-hatred! Plead the blood of Jesus upon our children. The enemy taunts us daily telling us that there is nothing we can do. The devil is a liar!

What would happen if **we** lifted our communities and rebuked satan, IN THE NAME OF JESUS, everyday at an assigned time? Would we see satan fall from the sky like lightning? I dare us to take a stand.

Communities: Pray

What other nation is so great as to have their gods near them the way the LORD our God is near us whenever we pray to him?
Deuteronomy 4: 7 (NIV)

Be unceasing in prayer [praying perseveringly];
1 Thessalonians 5:17 (AMP)

"How long will we continue praying for our communities?"

We are accustomed to deadlines and time-lines, but God's word tells us to pray **unceasingly; perseveringly; continually**.
 Consider this…
The LORD said to Satan, "Where have you come from?"
Satan answered the LORD, "From roaming throughout the earth, going back and forth on it." Job 1:7

The enemy does not put a time-line on his attacks, so let's not put one on our intercession. You may be led to pray for the week, month, 21-40 days, or until the enemy is done roaming…pray as the Holy Spirit leads you. The Lord did not specify a time, He simply said, "Pray".

Communities: Remove the obstacles

> [14] *And it will be said:"Build up, build up, prepare the road!*
> **Remove the obstacles out of the way of my people."**
> [15] *For this is what the high and exalted One says—*
> *he who lives forever, whose name is holy: "I live in a high*
> *and holy place, but also with the one who is contrite and*
> *lowly in spirit, to revive the spirit of the lowly and to revive*
> *the heart of the contrite.*
> *Isaiah 57: 14-15 (NIV)*

Do you ever see those who live in impoverished communities as being broken hearted and depressed over their situation?
Do you ever think of what it must be like to live in an area that negatively makes the news at least once a week?
Can you imagine the hopelessness one might feel? It's like "dry bones".

God is there! We don't see it with our natural eyes, but God's word tells us over and over that He is with the contrite (broken hearted) and lowly of spirit. He's waiting to redeem them. He wants to revive them!
Verse 14 helps us to focus our prayers for our communities and youth... *"Remove the obstacles out of the way of my people."*

What obstacles?
drug and alcohol abuse,
physical, sexual, emotional, verbal and psychological abuse,
lack (quality education, health care, healthy choices, inspiration, etc...),
violence,
etc...

Pray for these obstacles to be removed. It is easy to sit and judge the situation from afar; on the opposite side of our television screen. But when God blesses you to get close (it is a blessing)...You will see that many can not see past their situation, so they live according to what they see. We leave at the end of the day - they do not. So, we pray and trust God to do what He said He would do in the way *only He* can do.

Communities: Called and anointed

¹ The Spirit of the Sovereign Lord is upon me,
for the Lord has anointed me
to bring good news to the poor.
He has sent me to comfort the brokenhearted
and to proclaim that captives will be released
and prisoners will be freed.
² He has sent me to tell those who mourn
that the time of the Lord's favor has come,
and with it, the day of God's anger against their enemies.
³ To all who mourn in Israel,
*he will give **a crown of beauty** for ashes,*
***a joyous blessing** instead of mourning,*
***festive praise** instead of despair.*
In their righteousness, they will be like great oaks
that the Lord has planted for his own glory.
Isaiah 61: 1-3 (NLT)

We have been called and anointed to pray for the promises above. I believe and receive the call to intercede for our communities. In the name of Jesus, they will be revived! We are more than conquerors through Him that loves us.

Set apart

[22] "Your eye is a lamp that provides light for your body. When your eye is good, your whole body is filled with light. [23] But when your eye is bad, your whole body is filled with darkness. And if the light you think you have is actually darkness, how deep that darkness is!
Matthew 6: 22-23 (NLT)

[10] We have been set apart as holy because Jesus Christ did what God wanted him to do by sacrificing his body once and for all.
Hebrews 10: 10 (GW)

[21] So whoever cleanses himself [from what is ignoble and unclean, who separates himself from contact with contaminating and corrupting influences] will [then himself] be a vessel set apart and useful for honorable and noble purposes, consecrated and profitable to the Master, fit and ready for any good work.
2 Timothy 2: 21 (AMP)

When our daughter was younger, we permitted her to monitor her television programming by checking the ratings. If it was PG 13 or PG 14, she would ask before watching. Her dad and I would read the description and decide if she could watch it. We would also make sure we popped in to see what was going on or turn it on another television and watch for ourselves. We did this without her knowing, not because we didn't trust her, but because there is content that she didn't understand. Unfortunately, I've heard things spoken on programs that are rated for a younger audience but are completely unacceptable; children disrespecting their parents and parents being made to look like fools. Pre-teen and teenage girls obsessed with their looks and boys. I know society wants us to believe that's the way it is, but we are set apart and so are our children. We don't need society to shape our children.

So, what about our television intake as adults?
Are we watching programs that value who we are as men and women in Christ? What are the women like on the show? Are they like the adulterous woman of Proverbs 5 or honorable like the woman of Proverbs 31? The Proverbs 31 woman is a lofty goal, but I'd rather aim dignity than desperation.
Are we watching programs that value our men or are we laughing at what fools they are or are we disgusted by their immorality (yet watching)? How does that honor the man God has blessed me with…We don't need those thoughts and images in our minds.

Are we watching programs that uplift families or are we viewing dysfunction in every scene/episode?
We don't need society to shape *neither* our children *nor* us.

I find the questions above to be a little bothersome. I'd love to say that I don't struggle with the television programs I watch, but that would be a lie. I'm clear on obvious shows, but like children, there is inappropriate content we are not alert to. Honestly, there are some things we know about, but our flesh enjoys. We have a Father that monitors and prompts us for what we are blind to and not so blind to.

Faith and purpose

Arise, shine; for thy light is come, and the glory of the LORD
is risen upon thee.
Isaiah 60: 1 (KJV)

Isaiah 60: 1 is a call; a beckoning for us to step fearlessly into
God's purpose. "Step fearlessly" because the thought of
releasing control, even to the Lord, for some of us is scary.
When we begin to walk in His purpose things begin to happen.
We allow Him to remove the trash and clutter from our lives
and we see more clearly. We feel God moving in and through
us. The Lord begins to speak, or should I say, we begin to hear
and listen. We can't explain what He is doing because we don't
know. All we know is that we are becoming in tune with our
Lord. There is no need for us to be afraid because unlike the
"world", God ONLY has our best in mind. So, even if we don't
understand, we know we can trust God.

Burning

But if I say I'll never mention the Lord or speak in his name, **his word burns in my heart like a fire. It's like a fire in my bones!** *I am worn out trying to hold it in! I can't do it!*
Jeremiah 20: 9 (NLT)

"It's like fire shut up in my bones and I can't hold it in!" is what I have heard people say when they feel so full of the Holy Spirit that they just couldn't keep it in. I have referenced it when describing an encounter. Unfortunately, we get caught up on the imagery of the verse and lose the power of it.

We can't fully grasp the significance of the fire within Jeremiah without acknowledging the whole story. Jeremiah has bad news all the time because he has been called to prophesy God's judgment on an unrepentant nation. Nobody likes bad news especially folks uninterested in making amends, so he was persecuted. Prior to him crying out to the Lord, he was beaten and put in stocks (this order came from the priest Pashhur, 20:1-6). Upon his release the next day, he starts right back with his prophecy of God's judgment on Pashhur and his household. Jeremiah was commanded, by God, not to marry, so he didn't have a wife to go home to for comfort. Verses 7-8 show his frustration with God and his call. He talks about the ridicule, insult and reproach he receives all day. He talks about the proclamations of destruction he speaks. Then we get to our famous verse 9. Jeremiah contemplates keeping his mouth shut, but knows he can't. He's much too full of God's word and the call God has on his life is much too strong. This is not the first time he cries out in dismay to the Lord, but even in his frustration, he trusts God. He knows the character of God.

I began to think to myself…Do I really know what it is like to have fire *shut* up in my bones? Do I know what it is like to be persecuted, yet still proclaim God's message or is this a holy cliche?

Authentic worship

*When he reached the place where the road started down the Mount of Olives, all of his followers began to shout and sing as they walked along, praising God for all the wonderful miracles **they had seen**.*
Luke 19: 37 (NLT)

*Now when Herod saw Jesus, he was exceedingly glad, for he had eagerly desired to see Him for a long time because of what he had heard concerning Him, and he was hoping to witness some sign (some striking evidence or **spectacular performance**) done by Him.*
Luke 23: 8 (AMP)

It is so disturbing to read how some of the same followers who cried "Blessed", cried "Crucify" four chapters later. These were followers of Jesus, and one wonders how you go from being a follower of Christ to a hater. God showed me three words, "they had seen". They praised God for what they had seen. They were filled by what they saw; their flesh was fulfilled through the entertainment of watching. We do love a good show, don't we...?

Those who cried for Jesus' blood were no different than Herod. He, too, enjoyed a good show. When he didn't get what he wanted, he dismissed Jesus (Luke 23: 9-11)! Did the fair-weather followers not get what they wanted? Had they seen so many miracles that they expected a "Holy Show Down" between Jesus and those opposing Him? Were they looking for Warrior Angels killing in Jesus' defense, and when it didn't happen, they dismissed Him?...They didn't want the Lion and the Lamb - only the Lion??

Authentic praise comes from authentic relationship. Authentic relationship comes from moving beyond what we see and hear to what we know. What we have seen and heard does not sustain us when life does not play out like we want. Like Jeremiah, the fire within comes from knowing the character of God and trusting Him.

2011

God's will

³¹ Taking the twelve disciples aside, Jesus said, "Listen, we're going up to Jerusalem, where all the predictions of the prophets concerning the Son of Man will come true. ³² He will be handed over to the Romans, and he will be mocked, treated shamefully, and spit upon. ³³ They will flog him with a whip and kill him, but on the third day he will rise again."
³⁴ But they didn't understand any of this. The significance of his words was hidden from them, and they failed to grasp what he was talking about.
Luke 18: 31-34 (NLT)

It takes discipline to follow God's will. How many opportunities were there for Jesus' last days to end differently? None, but I used to wonder…
Could Judas have changed his mind about the betrayal and hung himself before identifying Jesus?
Could Pilate have been bold and refused to allow innocent blood to be shed?
Could the Pharisees and leaders have been doers of the word and not just hearers (i guess they actually were doers of the word)?

These questions are very child-like, but the flesh causes us to be child-like and not consider the big picture. The flesh denies the will of God in order to feel good for the moment. I read about the brutality Jesus faced and want to make changes to the story because it hurts my heart. Scripture was fulfilled for my/our benefit, for God's glory! Jesus suffered for **every** sin I have and will commit. Reflecting on His love can help us discipline ourselves to stay in the will of God.

Wisdom

32 Two other men, both criminals, were also led out with him to be executed. 33 When they came to the place called the Skull, they crucified him there, along with the criminals—one on his right, the other on his left.

39 One of the criminals who hung there hurled insults at him: "Aren't you the Messiah? Save yourself and us!"
40 But the other criminal rebuked him. "Don't you fear God," he said, "since you are under the same sentence? 41 We are punished justly, for we are getting what our deeds deserve. But this man has done nothing wrong."
42 Then he said, "Jesus, remember me when you come into your kingdom."
43 Jesus answered him, "Truly I tell you, today you will be with me in paradise."
Luke 23: 32-33, 39-43 (NIV)

7The reverent and worshipful fear of the Lord is the beginning and the principal and choice part of knowledge [its starting point and its essence];
***but** fools despise skillful and godly Wisdom, instruction, and discipline.*
Proverbs 1: 7

These two criminals can represent each part of Proverbs 1: 7; one wise and the other foolish. What can we learn about/from these two?
The *foolish* man was aware of his sin, *but* believed God owed him salvation. This is the person that thinks forgiveness is a license to sin again.
The *wise* man showed us three things:

1. a fear of God - reverence
2. an understanding of his own sinfulness - confession
3. a desire to be in close relationship with Jesus Christ - repentance

A sinner, saved by grace, was hours from hell, until Jesus! We, too, were knocking on hell's door, UNTIL JESUS! Hallelujah!

It is interesting that Jesus' final hours were spent much like His life's ministry; mockers and believers on each side.

Grace and mercy

God's mercy and grace are why we are not "getting what our deeds deserve".

What do our deeds deserve? Death

What do we get through Christ? Everlasting life

Romans 6: 23 (AMP)
For the wages which sin pays is death, **but** *the [bountiful] free gift of God is eternal life through (in union with) Jesus Christ our Lord.*

Looking for Jesus

¹ On the first day of the week, very early in the morning, the women took the spices they had prepared and went to the tomb. ²They found the stone rolled away from the tomb, ³ but when they entered, they did not find the body of the Lord Jesus. ⁴ While they were wondering about this, suddenly two men in clothes that gleamed like lightning stood beside them. ⁵ In their fright the women bowed down with their faces to the ground, but the men said to them, "Why do you look for the living among the dead? **⁶He is not here; he has risen!** *Remember how he told you, while he was still with you in Galilee: ⁷ 'The Son of Man must be delivered over to the hands of sinners, be crucified and on the third day be raised again.' " ⁸ Then they remembered his words.*

²¹ but we had hoped that he was the one who was going to redeem Israel. And what is more, it is the third day since all this took place. ²² In addition, some of our women amazed us. They went to the tomb early this morning ²³ but didn't find his body. They came and told us that they had seen a vision of angels, who said he was alive. ²⁴ Then some of our companions went to the tomb and found it just as the women had said, but they did not see Jesus."

³⁰ When he was at the table with them, he took bread, gave thanks, broke it and began to give it to them. ³¹ **Then their eyes were opened and they recognized him,** *and he disappeared from their sight.*
Luke 24: 1-8, 21-24, 30-31 (NIV)

The only thing predictable about Jesus is His love for us and His word! Verses 1-8 show us that He is not always found in the places we look for Him to be, and verses 21-24 show us that Jesus can be upon us while we are thinking (or verbalizing) He hasn't shown up. Only our Lord has us covered by walking steps ahead, behind, alongside, and/or carrying us according to our needs.

Regardless of where you are looking or what road you are on, these two passages provide us peace in knowing:
He is risen! (v 1-8)
He is with us! (v 21-24)

Invitation

*[28] As they approached the village to which they were going, Jesus continued on **as if** he were going farther. [29] But they urged him strongly, "Stay with us, for it is nearly evening; the day is almost over." So he went in to stay with them.*
[30] When he was at the table with them, he took bread, gave thanks, broke it and began to give it to them.
[31] Then their eyes were opened and they recognized him, and he disappeared from their sight.

I am convinced that Jesus continued on "as if" he were going further, so they could invite Him to stay and He could reveal Himself to them. Isn't that what it takes? We ask Jesus into our hearts; He comes, stays, and reveals Himself.

He already inhabited their hearts; they just needed to see Him in a new "light". We can become accustomed to seeing Jesus in one way, and miss Him when He shows up differently. The two disciples were close to a breakthrough, they didn't know what, but they knew they were not ready for their guest to leave. So, they pursued their breakthrough by inviting Him to stay. Thank God, Jesus lingers close so we can reach out and grab anew! The key is to pursue and invite Jesus in.

Be imitators: Every opportunity

THEREFORE BE imitators of God [copy Him and follow His example],... *Be very careful, then, how you live—not as unwise but as wise,* **making the most of every opportunity**, *because the days are evil.*
Ephesians 5: 1 (AMP), 15-16 (NIV)

What opportunity? EVERY opportunity... For what? To be *imitators* of God!

We must be careful and wise whether at work, the grocery store, in line to pay a bill, in traffic court, or on the phone with a disgruntled individual. The first verse of this chapter begins with "Therefore Be imitators of God,". There were no time or situational constraints placed on these words. We know it is not a suggestion, but a directive. We must make the most of every opportunity to imitate God. God has caused me to ask myself a few questions when I don't want to do something or go somewhere:
What is it God wants me to receive?
What is it the enemy is trying to keep from me?

After all, it's easy to imitate God when we are doing, going and saying what we want. It's when my flesh rises up I have to "imitate" God. I have to pray for my flesh to be pushed down in order to walk in His way. I have begun to wonder why my flesh resists some opportunities... What might I miss out on? Could it be a divine appointment? I am often reminded that this life is not about me.

Years ago, a woman said she thought it was fanatical to try to see God in "each and every little opportunity or circumstance".

There are many in agreement with that thought, but I contend that until we learn to see God in every facet of life - we will have a dull view.

Be imitators: Whatever happens

[27] **Whatever happens**, *conduct yourselves in a manner worthy of the gospel of Christ.*
Philippians 1:27a (NIV)

"Whatever happens" is a tall order!
Those first two words are confirmation that we have no control over anything. The New Living Translation reads, "Above all,…" These phrases help me to keep in mind that being a reflection of God is the most important thing I can do all day.

When I meditate on being an imitator of God and making the most of every opportunity, I can add today's verse. So, when the gas station attendant is rude, we are still called to reflect Christ. When falsely accused, we are to reflect Christ. When receiving accolades, we are to reflect Christ.

It is difficult to read, pray, and study the words God inspired Paul to write without considering his location at the time. Paul was in prison, yet encouraged his brothers and sisters in Christ.
 "Whatever happens…"

Forward

* Brothers and sisters, I do not consider myself yet to have taken hold of it. But one thing I do: Forgetting what is behind and straining toward what is ahead, I press on toward the goal to win the prize for which God has called me heavenward in Christ Jesus. All of us, then, who are mature should take such a view of things. And if on some point you think differently, that too God will make clear to you.*
Philippians 3:13-15 (NIV)

It takes maturity in Christ and perseverance to forget your past and move forward.
The enemy would like to have kept Paul a self-righteous murder accomplice, but God had other plans. Defeated, yet again, the accuser would have enjoyed hindering Paul's ministry by keeping his mind in bondage because of his past. Verses 13-15 conquers self-destructive thoughts. Paul doesn't just move forward, he strains and presses forward. He also forgets the past.

How could he have forgotten such treachery? He didn't allow his thoughts about the past to consume him. He knew three things and we would do well to grasp them ourselves.

1. He knew his sins were forgotten and forgiven.
"He has removed our sins as far from us as the east is from the west."
Psalm 103:12 (NLT)

2. He knew how much God loved him.
may have power, together with all the Lord's holy people, to grasp how wide and long and high and deep is the love of Christ, and to know

this love that surpasses knowledge—that you may be filled to the measure of all the fullness of God." Ephesians 3:18-19 (NIV)

3. He knew he didn't have to understand God's love (it's not humanly possible to), but he could grasp and accept it.
 Ephesians 3:19

What are you *choosing* to hold on to?
If you have asked for forgiveness and repented, it is already nailed to the cross. Quit taking it down and nursing it back to life! Forget it, press on, and grasp the Love that surpasses all understanding!

Light

*14"You are light **for** the world. A city cannot be hidden when it is located on a hill. 15No one lights a lamp and puts it under a basket. Instead, everyone who lights a lamp puts it on a lamp stand. Then its light shines on everyone in the house. 16In the same way let your light shine in front of people. Then they will see the good that you do and praise your Father in heaven.*
Matthew 5: 14-16 (GW)

The use of "light **for** the world" instead of "light **of** the world" puts our purpose in perspective. What do a city located on a hill and a lamp on a lampstand have in common? They are both set apart. God created and set us apart to be light in dark places. God places us in positions so He can illuminate us! As we light the way for others, shine for God's glory and don't worry about what anyone else says or thinks. When God's anointing is upon you, you become a reflection of Him. We were made for others.

Instead

Instead, be filled with the Spirit,...
Ephesians 5:18b (NIV)

The need to fill implies an emptiness or void. We all have times when we feel an emptiness or void in our lives. Although this verse is specific to alcohol consumption (read the verse in its entirety), it applies to all things we would use to fill us during those times of emptiness. As humans, we have a tendency to fill ourselves with "stuff" that satisfies our flesh, but not our spirit. Food, drink, entertainment, people, and things (material, jobs, titles, etc…) temporarily get the job done, but then what? Instead of fillers, we must grab hold to that which will fulfill us. To fill means to make full, but to fulfill means to carry out or bring to realization. Being fulfilled by the Spirit of God leads us to carry out the plans He has for us to glorify Him.

The power of our testimony

The power of the woman's testimony is not that Jesus told her everything she ever did. What she "did" was no secret…she previously had five husbands and at the time of their meeting, was living with a man. Her deeds were known. In fact, that is why she was at the well during the time Jesus was there. She was avoiding what everyone knew.

The power of her testimony (and ours) is that Jesus loved and offered her everlasting life *in spite of* what she did or was doing. If you read back to their meeting (verses 13-18), Jesus does not reveal that He knows her history until **after** He offers her the Living Water. Sin is sin - Jesus is not interested in the details of our sin, but in the details of our salvation. Jesus' time and words are spent on bringing her into relationship with Him, not on condemning what they both knew she was guilty of.

God is good and His love is perfect. This woman, who at one time switched her daily schedule to avoid ridicule, was now testifying to everyone in the village. The fear she once carried was gone because she experienced the perfect love of Christ.

Testify to encourage

29"Come with me, and meet a man who told me everything I've ever done. Could he be the Messiah?"
John 4: 29 (GW), 39-42 (NLT)

39 Many Samaritans from the village believed in Jesus because the woman had said, "He told me everything I ever did!"
*40 When they came out to see him, they begged him to stay in their village. So he stayed for two days, 41 long enough for many more to hear his message and believe. 42 Then they said to the woman, "Now we believe, **not just because** of what you told us, **but because we have heard him ourselves**. **Now we know** that he is indeed the Savior of the world."*

The Samaritans and Jews had a long history of dislike and disdain toward each other. It dated all the way back to the Old Testament and was as fresh as Luke 9: 52-53. What an awesome testimony and message this woman had to have had for the Samaritans to seek a Jew, by the name of Jesus Christ.

Our testimonies ought to encourage others to *taste and see that the Lord is good*. When we point others to Jesus, they invite Him to stay awhile and are fulfilled!

"Now we believe, not just because of what you told us, but because we have heard him ourselves. Now we know that he is indeed the Savior of the world."

Crossing boundaries

When a Samaritan woman came to draw water, Jesus said to her, "Will you give me a drink?"
John 4: 7 (NIV)

We don't know her name, yet "Samaritan woman" tells us everything we need to know about Jesus.
She represents the boundaries that our Lord will cross to give the gift of life:

- She comes from "the wrong side of town". *Samaria...*
- She is considered weak. *A woman...*
- She goes against societal norms. *Her relationship status (past and present), talking to a Jewish man, and being at the well at noon...*

We may not relate to her story because we think Jesus did not cross those same boundaries to get to us, but look again.

Let's compare stories:

- Did you **live** in sin?
- Were you **weak** to sin?
- Did you **challenge the love of God** through your sin?

I don't know about you, but my answers make me want to leave my water jar and go tell some folks about the Man I met!

TRUNK

the trunk connects the roots with its crown

Speak life

*3In these lay a great number of sick folk--some blind, some
crippled, and some paralyzed (shriveled up)--waiting for the
bubbling up of the water. 4For an angel of the Lord went down
at appointed seasons into the pool and moved and stirred up
the water; whoever then first, after the stirring up of the
water, stepped in was cured of whatever disease with which he
was afflicted. 5There was a certain man there who had suffered
with a deep-seated and lingering disorder for thirty-eight
years. 6When Jesus noticed him lying there [helpless], knowing
that he had already been a long time in that condition, He
said to him,* **Do you want to become well?** *[Are you
really in earnest about getting well?] 7The invalid answered,
Sir, I have nobody when the water is moving to put me into the
pool; but while I am trying to come [into it] myself, somebody
else steps down ahead of me. 8Jesus said to him, Get up! Pick
up your bed (sleeping pad) and walk! 9Instantly the man
became well and recovered his strength and picked up his bed
and walked.*
John 5: 3-9 (AMP)

Hallelujah! I am so happy Jesus will bless us in spite of us!
8Jesus said to him, Get up! Pick up your bed (sleeping pad) and walk!

Thirty-eight years…The man had been in "that" condition for
thirty-eight years.
What condition? The condition of being an invalid physically
and <u>invalid</u> (not valid) mentally. The man had taken up
residence by a healing pool, yet when asked if he wanted to
become well, he reported that he had been passed by and
stepped over.

⁷The invalid answered, Sir, I have nobody when the water is moving to put me into the pool; but while I am trying to come [into it] myself, somebody else steps down ahead of me.

Really sir, that's your answer? He didn't know **Jesus** was asking, but what if this was someone who wanted to carry him to the pool for his blessing (advancement)?? He was so consumed with not being healed (advanced) that had it not been for the goodness of Jesus, he would have died an invalid.

Speak life. Watch your words and always anticipate a blessing. Some of us are like the invalid. We get so caught up in what's not right that we miss blessing after blessing. Who knows who the Lord has sent our way to bless us, but by the time we get done talking about how we got passed over for the promotion or how we wanted to go back to school, but the economy is so bad…the person may move on. Next time someone asks you a question about advancement (isn't that the question Jesus asks), skip the excuses and speak your blessings. "Yes, I want to be well. I want to walk and run! I want to soar!"

God is good, but we have to believe and receive His goodness!
2011

Anger at God

2This Mary was the one who anointed the Lord with perfume and wiped His feet with her hair. It was her brother Lazarus who was [now] sick. 5Now Jesus loved Martha and her sister and Lazarus. [They were His dear friends, and He held them in loving esteem.] 20When Martha heard that Jesus was coming, she went to meet Him, while Mary remained sitting in the house. 32When Mary came to the place where Jesus was and saw Him, she dropped down at His feet, saying to Him, Lord, if You had been here, my brother would not have died.
John 11: 2, 5, 20, 32 (AMP)

John goes out of his way to teach us a lesson through Mary. John makes three very significant points:
- This is the same Mary that anoints Jesus' feet with oil. John doesn't officially write about it until chapter 12, but considers it crucial to mention in chapter 11.
- Jesus loved her, her sister and her brother. Didn't Jesus love everyone?
- Mary stayed at home when she heard Jesus was coming.

It's all significant because Mary is angry with Jesus. She doesn't sin in her anger, she just stays home with no intentions of talking to Him. She's respectful and goes when He calls, but she really doesn't want to be bothered with Jesus.

Her anger is much deeper than her brother's death. People die every day, but **she** called on Jesus and He did not show up. The root of her anger and ours, when we find ourselves in an angry season, sprouts from two places: relationship and faith!

Relationship - She felt she should receive special treatment because of the closeness of her relationship with the Lord. She and her siblings had a very dear relationship with Jesus. They spent as much time together as possible.

For example: You go to Bible Study every week and you teach Sunday School. You serve on the Deacon Board and the intercessory prayer team. Yet, when you called on Jesus to save your child, He didn't show up.

Faith - She knew He was MORE than able, so why didn't He save Lazarus... He delivered her. He was able to say a word without being in the same location and people were healed. He healed a man who was blind from birth. Why not Lazarus?

For example: You watch the HGTV channel and see all these young people buying beautiful homes. You look at their age and their income and it doesn't add up that they are buying these home and you are still in an apartment. You know God is able - you've testified to His goodness! He's awesome, so when is your blessing going to come...

She's angry and I get it. God didn't say we wouldn't be angry, He told us not to sin in our anger (Ephesians 4:26). So, what do we do when we are angry and don't know how to make it right? I don't know, but what I do know is that the next story John tells about Mary is that she is anointing Jesus' feet with oil and wiping his feet with her hair. Her "season" of anger came to an end. John didn't say, "After three months, Mary came around and was no longer angry with Jesus." Had the time frame been relevant, I'm sure John would've shared it.

We can learn three things from Mary.
We will be angry with God.
Our anger is often rooted in our relationship with Him and our faith in Him.
When we have relationship and faith, our "angry season" WILL come to an end. (The devil is a liar!)

Beware

³ Then Mary took about a pint of pure nard, an expensive perfume; she poured it on Jesus' feet and wiped his feet with her hair. **And the house was filled with the fragrance of the perfume.** *⁴ But one of his disciples, Judas Iscariot, who was later to betray him, objected, ⁵ "Why wasn't this perfume sold and the money given to the poor? It was worth a year's wages."⁶ He did not say this because he cared about the poor…*
⁷ **"Leave her alone,"** *Jesus replied.*
John 12: 3 - 6a, 7a (NIV)

Be alert, there is a Judas in your midst. The sweet fragrance of your praise and worship is more than he/she can take. Your praise to some is contagious and they reflect on the goodness of the Lord, but to others it is offensive.

Judas is offended because Jesus is someone he is hanging out with until a better opportunity comes along, but for Mary - Jesus is her all. There is no better opportunity ahead; she's tried and knows. She's seen what He can do and what He won't do. She's been angry with Him and reconciled her feelings to anoint His feet and use her hair to wipe them. Jesus is her everything and she doesn't concern herself with what anyone thinks about "how" she shows it.

There will always be those who question our praise, our worship, our devotion and our love for Christ. Be alert so that you are knowledgeable of what spirit is in your environment, but you don't have to deal with it. Jesus is our defender!

Go and get your "praise on". Jesus will tell the naysayers "Leave her/him alone."

Pride: Your true identity

*¹ Some time later King Xerxes promoted Haman son of Hammedatha the Agagite over all the other nobles, making him the most powerful official in the empire. ² All the king's officials would bow down before Haman to show him respect whenever he passed by, **for so the king had commanded. But Mordecai refused** to bow down or show him respect. ⁹ Haman was a happy man as he left the banquet! But when he saw Mordecai sitting at the palace gate, not standing up or trembling nervously before him, Haman became furious. ¹⁰ However, he restrained himself and went on home. Then Haman gathered together his friends and Zeresh, his wife, ¹¹ and boasted to them about his great wealth and his many children. He bragged about the honors the king had given him and how he had been promoted over all the other nobles and officials. ¹² Then Haman added, "And that's not all! Queen Esther invited only me and the king himself to the banquet she prepared for us. And she has invited me to dine with her and ¹³ Then he added, **"But this is all worth nothing as long as I see Mordecai the Jew just sitting there at the palace gate."***
Esther 5: 3: 1-2; 9-13 (NLT)

The King promoted Haman as the most powerful official in the empire, yet Mordecai had greater power. His power was not in his position, but in his ability to ruin Haman's day!

Haman was feeling good about being Haman until he saw Mordecai. I imagine him walking along, pep in his step, head held high - he may have been whistling, until he laid eyes on Mordecai. Verse 9 reads that he became "furious" when he saw him sitting at the palace gate and in verse 13 he says it all means nothing as long as he sees Mordecai. He hated Mordecai and it came from deep within. With all of the power he had, he lacked self-esteem. His hatred for Mordecai also caused him to be foolish. He spent energy against him when he didn't have to. If we go back to verse 2 of the third chapter, the king commanded that everyone bow down. Mordecai refused, so why not report him to the king?

Haman's esteem was in his position and Mordecai's was in God. *¹ What is causing the quarrels and fights among you? Don't they come from the evil desires at war within you? ² You want what you don't have, so you scheme and kill to get it. You are jealous of what others have, but you can't get it, so you fight and wage war to take it away from them. Yet you don't have what you want because you don't ask God for it.* James 4:1-2

Haman can't ask because he doesn't know God. He is his own god. This serves to remind us of the importance of knowing God and finding our identity in Him.

Pride: Who's holding you accountable?

> *⁹Harbona, one of the eunuchs present with the king, said, "What a coincidence! The 75-foot pole Haman made for Mordecai, who spoke up for the well-being of the king, is still standing at Haman's house." The king responded, "Hang him on it!" ¹⁰So servants hung Haman's dead body on the very pole he had prepared for Mordecai. Then the king got over his raging anger.*
> Esther 7: 9-10 (GW)

It is impossible to study the story of Haman without looking at his downfall. The gallows or pole he built for Mordecai was his destination. It doesn't pay to build gallows, dig holes, or set traps for others; it will always come back to you.
²⁷Whoever digs a pit [for another man's feet] shall fall into it himself, and he who rolls a stone [up a height to do mischief], it will return upon him.
Proverbs 26: 27 (AMP)

Believe it or not, Haman's story holds another lesson for us.
*¹⁴Then **his wife Zeresh and all his friends** said to him, "Have a pole set up, 75 feet high, and in the morning ask the king to have Mordecai's dead body hung on it. Then go with the king to the dinner in good spirits."*
  Haman liked the idea, so he had the pole set up. Esther 5: 14 (GW)

Who is in your inner circle? Do they hold you accountable for righteousness or so they co-sign your foolishness?
In chapter 5, Haman boasts to his circle, then ends it with a statement revealing his true insecurity. Someone should have asked why, with all of his *greatness*, was he so focused on

Mordecai or pulled him aside to discuss his obvious heart issues. Instead, they (wife and friends) suggested he have Mordecai killed, have dinner and be happy. I'm sure Haman was more than capable of devising his own treacherous scheme, but hey - what are friends for?

12... but Haman hurried home dejected and completely humiliated.
*13 When Haman told his wife, Zeresh, and all his friends what had happened, his wise advisers and his wife said, "**Since Mordecai— this man who has humiliated you—is of Jewish birth, you will never succeed in your plans against him. It will be fatal to continue opposing him.**"* Esther 6:12-13 (NLT)

Proverbs 27:17 advises us to find some "iron" friends to keep us sharp. If you have a circle that love you enough to tell you the truth about your behavior, praise God!
If not, pray for some! Look at where the advice of Haman's inner circle landed him.

Speak life

14 From the fruit of their lips people are filled with good things,…
Proverbs 12:14a (NIV)

The words we speak should be refreshing and nourishing like fresh fruit. People should see us coming and anticipate something good coming from our lips.

In contrast, what do you do when you the negative complainer headed your way? You pause like a trapped animal and begin thinking of an escape from what you know you are about to hear. If possible, you will wave and go find that "thing" you "forgot" on the other side of the building. If you are trapped, you know you are going to have to do some praying and rebuking to rid yourself of the poison.

People who speak life, have life and give life.

Serving

*³ Jesus knew that the Father had given him complete power; he knew that he had come from God and was going to God.⁴ **So** he rose from the table, took off his outer garment, and tied a towel around his waist.⁵ Then he poured some water into a washbasin and began to wash the disciples' feet and dry them with the towel around his waist.*
John 13:3-5 (GNT)

Serving for the Lord is an act of worship that we often take for granted. We *serve* for various reasons: fun activities, tradition, high profile, etc…

Jesus teaches us an important lesson about service.
Righteous servants:
Know their Power Source is the Lord.
Know who they are IN the Lord.
Know where they are going IN the Lord.
Lastly, they are able to take off the exteriors (titles, degrees, etc…) and "wash feet".

Verse 3 tells us what Jesus knew, and then the first word in verse 4 is, "So". It was natural for Jesus to know who He was **and** serve. It also allowed Him, the Son of God, to wash feet. Think of Jesus the next time you are called to serve.

Healing #1

As I studied in the book of John, I found it interesting how Jesus healed through commands. If you read about the invalid (38 years by the pool), the man blind from birth, and Lazarus' death, you will note that Jesus always tells them to **do** something. God showed me that Jesus' healing manifests itself differently according to the situation. They are all called to move forward, but the follow up differs.

We will look at the spiritually crippled, spiritually blind, and spiritually dead. We'll study the first today and the other two separately. The spiritually blind and dead require a great deal more attention (if you've ever been there…you know it's true).

- The spiritually crippled are called to get up and walk away from their place of *waiting*.
- The spiritually blind are called to wash in the Spirit of the One who was "sent".
- The spiritually dead are called to have their *death clothes* removed.

Spiritually Crippled

8 Jesus told him, "Stand up, pick up your mat, and walk!"
14 But afterward Jesus found him in the Temple and told him,
"Now you are well; so stop sinning, or something even worse
may happen to you."
John 5: 8, 14 (NLT)

Those of us who are or have been spiritually crippled often stay because we do not move. Not only do we stay, we blame. The only way to move is to be obedient to Jesus' words.
Verse 14 is a caution…Once you have been healed of your impairment or weakened state, don't go back to visit it or you will find yourself sinning and in a worsened condition. Jesus told the man to pick up his belongings and walk. He had all he needed: the Power to move, his belongings, and direction; no need to turn back.
2011

Healing #2

Jesus' healing manifests itself differently according to the situation.

The spiritually blind are called to wash in the Spirit of the One who was "sent".

Spiritually Blind

⁷ He told him, "Go wash yourself in the pool of Siloam" **(Siloam means "sent").** *So the man went and washed and came back seeing!⁸ His neighbors and others who knew him as a blind beggar asked each other, "Isn't this the man who used to sit and beg?" ⁹Some said he was, and others said, "No, he just looks like him!"But the beggar kept saying, "Yes, I am the same one!"⁵ "I don't know whether he is a sinner," the man replied. "But I know this: I was blind, and now I can see!"* John 9: 7-9, 25 (NLT)

Like the man who had been blind since birth, Jesus allows us to become clean in Him (the One who was "Sent") and receive our sight . Jesus gives us sight as though we were blind. We begin to see differently, like for the first time. Not only do we receive sight, we also have a new appearance. In verses 8 and 9, his neighbors were trying to figure out who he was. He looked the same, but something was different and they were convinced it wasn't him. They were accustomed to him begging and reaching aimlessly.

Jesus gives us sight, a new appearance, and an unwavering testimony. He couldn't wait to tell what Jesus did for him ("Yes, I am the same one!"). Don't you feel the same way? Don't you want people to know, "Yes, I am the one who ...., but that is when I was blind. Look at what the Lord did for me!" Verses 13-24 document the attempts of the enemy to question his testimony and the authority of Jesus. The enemy does not want us to have sight and he becomes angry when we share our testimony. Check out the response of the one who has sight…*"I was blind, and now I can see!"* That is the bottom line!

Healing #3

Jesus' healing manifests itself differently according to the situation.

The spiritually dead are called to have their *death clothes* removed.

Spiritually Dead

⁴³ Then Jesus shouted, "Lazarus, come out!"
⁴⁴ And the dead man came out, his hands and feet bound in
graveclothes, his face wrapped in a headcloth.
Jesus told them, "Unwrap him and let him go!"
John 11: 43-44 (NLT)

The spiritually dead are brought back to life. They can come when Jesus calls, but are so deep in bondage that they require outside support. They need others to remove their "death clothes" before they can move any further. Lazarus' hands and feet were bound with burial linens/cloths and his face/head was covered. He couldn't walk too far and he couldn't remove the cloth himself. Spiritual death binds us in the same way; our movement is restricted (hands, feet, mind) and we need others.

This takes me back to our inner circle...Not only do we need people who will hold us accountable, but we also need:
Those unafraid of what God is doing in our lives. (Some will not be happy to see you come out of your tomb!)
Those not offended by the stench of death on us. We need folks who love us enough to help us remove what we are buried in, not turn up their noses and go the other way.

The spiritually crippled, blind, and dead all require Jesus Christ *and* the willingness to immediately obey His word.

God is able!

Wavering faith

²⁰ So they brought him. When the spirit saw Jesus, it immediately threw the boy into a convulsion. He fell to the ground and rolled around, foaming at the mouth.
²¹ Jesus asked the boy's father, "How long has he been like this?""From childhood," he answered. ²² "It has often thrown him into fire or water to kill him. But if you can do anything, take pity on us and help us."³ "'If you can'?" said Jesus. "Everything is possible for one who believes."
²⁴ Immediately the boy's father exclaimed,"I do believe; help me overcome my unbelief!"
Mark 9: 20-24 (NIV)

I can appreciate this man's request for Jesus to help his unbelief. Our faith causes us to seek Jesus, but sometimes what we have seen and experienced for so long shakes us. What had the man seen and experienced? He saw his son tormented and he experienced the failure of the followers of Jesus. the enemy knows which "flaming arrows" to throw, but Jesus shows up to strengthen our unbelief and extinguish the arrows!

There are times I need Jesus to help my unbelief and He is faithful to help me readjust my shield of faith, just as He did with the boy's father…

"Everything is possible for one who believes."

This man's admission of wavering faith lets me know I am not alone.

But Jesus!

^{22} Many times the evil spirit has tried to kill him by throwing him in the fire and into water...
^{26} The spirit screamed, threw the boy into a bad fit, and came out. The boy looked like a corpse, and everyone said, He is dead!^{27} But Jesus...took the boy by the hand and helped him rise, and he stood up.
Mark 9: 22a, 26-27 (GNT)

Those five words...! "He is dead! But Jesus..."
Despite how the enemy tormented this boy...Despite what it looked like...BUT JESUS!
If we could only remember "but Jesus" for ourselves and others.

God spoke two thoughts for these five words.
The first thought was if the enemy has ever tormented *or is* tormenting you, it is for the purpose of killing/destroying you.
 BUT JESUS...If you are reading this, the Lord has plans for you.
If people have looked at you or your situation, and have spoken death, BUT JESUS.
There's nothing more to say. **"Thank you Jesus!"**

The second thought was about when we count others out. I know it is easier to rejoice over BUT JESUS when we focus on how we have been tormented or counted out, but we have all spoken death to others. It doesn't feel good to admit, but sin shouldn't feel good. BUT JESUS...Who are we to call anything dead? It's not our place. Let's use our words to uplift.

Peace

Search for peace, and work to maintain it.
Psalm 34: 14b (NLT)

I struggled for peace this week, but was determined and made
the decision on Monday morning to strive for it. Well, of
course that was an invitation for battle with the enemy! I made
the decision on Monday, and God whispered a reminder on
Tuesday, "through Me". I gladly accepted His invitation to
fight my battle for peace. I stumbled a few times, but the Lord
didn't. I had to keep looking to Him and talking to Him aloud.
I had to talk to the enemy aloud, in the name of Jesus, as well.
All glory goes to God; He is faithful!

Look to God and keep your focus on Him, you will find and
maintain peace. It is possible to work in a hostile environment
and maintain our "light". It is possible to <u>not</u> know the
outcome, yet be secure. It is possible to be silent (keep your
peace) and show mercy to a person offending us.
All things are possible *through* our Lord!

The real meal

*29And He replied to them, **This kind** cannot be driven out by anything but prayer and fasting.*
Mark 9: 29 (AMP)

Fasting was a discipline the disciples had not yet begun, so when "This kind..." came, they were ill-prepared to deal with it. It was chaotic; they were surrounded and arguing with the teachers of the law. Jesus wasn't around (He was on the way, but they couldn't see him...) and their faith was not strong enough to stand against what was before them. Prayer and fasting fill and satisfy us when we are empty of the things the world says we must have to survive. Fasting fills us in such a way that when situations cause us to feel like He is not there or we don't see Him, our faith kicks in immediately.

We don't ever know when a "This kind..." situation will arise. Advance notice would be great, but things occur that we can NEVER be prepared for. Prayer and fasting position us so we are prepared IN and through God.

When we reserve fasting for special occasions, dilemmas, or favor trading with God (I won't eat this, if you give me that...), we miss out on the real meal!

Power of God

*So they brought the boy. But when the evil spirit **saw** Jesus, it **threw** the child into a violent convulsion, and he fell to the ground, writhing and foaming at the mouth.*
Mark 9: 20 (NLT)

How is it that demons **immediately** recognize Jesus and react to Him, but we are so slow?
Jesus is always in our midst, but somehow we miss Him. Then there are the times we clearly recognize Him, but fail to react appropriately. Of course, a child of God will not have the same reaction as a demon, but sometimes we do nothing. For example, God has healed the sickness in your body, but you are angry that you were sick in the first place. We fail to recognize and react appropriately to Jesus. Another example, you didn't get the position you want, so you wallow in rejection. You have a job which is much more than some can say. We fail to recognize and react appropriately to Jesus.

What is it that those evil spirits seem to know that we do not know...or seem to "forget"?
They know every knee shall bow and every tongue will confess that Jesus Christ is Lord.
They know when Jesus shows up, evil must flee.
In other words, they recognize and react to the power of Jesus. They recognize and react to the fact that they are powerless before our Lord.

Is that the problem with us? Do we desire so much power and control over our lives that we fail to recognize and react to Jesus or do we simply refuse? Do demons have more faith in the power of Jesus than us?

We can learn from 'Blind' Bartimaeus.

> [46] *Then they reached Jericho, and as Jesus and his disciples left town, a large crowd followed him. A blind beggar named Bartimaeus (son of Timaeus) was sitting beside the road.* [47] *When Bartimaeus **heard** that Jesus of Nazareth was nearby, **he began to shout**, "Jesus, Son of David, have mercy on me!"* [48] *"Be quiet!" many of the people yelled at him. **But he only shouted louder**, "Son of David, have mercy on me!"*
> *Mark 10: 46-48 NLT*

He heard, he shouted, he refused to be silenced! He was a blind beggar (physically powerless), but able to recognize and react to the power of Jesus...
We need to let go of our false sense of power, so we can recognize and react to Jesus in a way that gives glory to Him.

God's will

*[1] And so, dear brothers and sisters, I plead with you to give your bodies to God because of all he has done for you. Let them be a living and holy sacrifice—the kind he will find acceptable. This is truly the way to worship him. [2] Don't copy the behavior and customs of this world, but let God transform you into a new person by changing the way you think. Then you will learn to know God's will for you, which is **good and pleasing and perfect**.*
Romans 12:1-2 (NLT)

Good and pleasing and perfect to whom? To God!

Those three words are the reason why we must not conform to the patterns of this world and must allow God to change the way we think. In our flesh, those words mean, "I get what I want. I get it the way I want it and when I want it." I have made more poor decisions based on the world's view of those words. I was in alignment with the world's view - I wasn't forced. Once we learn to discern God's will, we learn that our growth is more important than our comfort. We learn that we are living sacrifices to glorify the Lord.

A few weeks ago, we visited a nursing home during dinner.
 Dinner was served and one of the more boisterous residents complained, "I wanted soup! I don't want this. I want soup!"

This went on for about five long minutes. The gentleman we were visiting looked up from his meal and quietly said, "You get what's on the menu."

He continued calmly eating his meal. I don't think I will ever forget that. I felt God was speaking directly to me because, "I want soup!"

God is the chef. He feeds us what we need to grow stronger, but we get what's on the menu. God's will is the menu and it will nourish us. We can only enjoy the meal when we change our thinking from what we want to what God wants.
(Little did I know that in three years, I would be visiting our father in a similar setting.)

Wisdom

Do not forsake wisdom, and she will protect you; love her, and she will watch over you.
Proverbs 4:6 (NLT)

Wisdom comes from God. It is interesting; some older dictionary versions define it as "common sense". We cannot confuse wisdom from God with worldly wisdom or common sense. There is nothing "common" about anything God gives, and make no mistake; wisdom is a gift.
Consider these common sense and wisdom scenarios:
Common sense tells us not to step in front of a bus.
Wisdom tells us to pray before stepping into a relationship.
Common sense helps us with things that are evident, but wisdom guides us where we cannot see.

Our flesh prefers foolishness; it is our nature to forsake wisdom. Foolishness is a tool of the enemy to kill/destroy us. The foolishness of the world seems like so much fun until the consequences kick in. Wisdom protects and guards us from tactics designed to harm us. Proverbs encourages us to strive for wisdom, "Blessed is the man who finds wisdom,…", "Get wisdom…", "Do not forsake wisdom,…", the list goes on.

[12]Wisdom will save you from the way of evil, from the person who speaks devious things, [13]from those who abandon the paths of righteousness to walk the ways of darkness, [14]from those who enjoy doing evil, from those who find joy in the deviousness of evil.
Proverbs 2:12-14 (GW)

Misinterpreted favor by a parent or guardian

> ¹SO JACOB dwelt in the land in which his father had been a stranger and sojourner, in the land of Canaan.
> ²This is the history of the descendants of Jacob and this is Jacob's line. Joseph, when he was seventeen years old, was shepherding the flock with his brothers; the lad was with the sons of Bilhah and Zilpah, his father's [secondary] wives; and Joseph brought to his father a bad report of them. ³**Now Israel loved Joseph more than all his children because he was the son of his old age, and he made him a [distinctive] long tunic with sleeves.** ⁴But when his brothers saw that their father loved [Joseph] more than all of his brothers, they hated him and could not say, Peace [in friendly greeting] to him or speak peaceably to him.
> Genesis 37:1-4 (AMP)

The misinterpretations of God's favor causes heartache to all involved. In the story of Joseph, we see three types of misinterpretations of God's favor: parental, others, and self.

Israel misinterpreted the favor of God upon Joseph as being something he did. Verse 3 states that he loved him more than the others because he was the son of his old age. Joseph was a reminder of Israel's virility, not of God's greatness. As a result, he raised him above the other sons causing him <u>and</u> them to feel that he (Joseph) was better. He caused strife between Joseph and his brothers. Instead of direction, discipline and guidance, he clothed Joseph with conceit and arrogance. This was the beginning of heartache.

God's favor is a gift; there's nothing we can do to earn it. It doesn't come with birth order, DNA, appearance or intellectual ability. As a parent or one entrusted with the guidance of another, we must not place God's favor on "earthly" terms. We have to recognize and honor the Source in order to direct those in our care on a path of righteousness.

Misinterpreted favor by others

[18] When Joseph's brothers saw him coming, they recognized him in the distance. As he approached, they made plans to kill him.[19] "Here comes the dreamer!" they said. [20] "Come on, let's kill him and throw him into one of these cisterns. We can tell our father, 'A wild animal has eaten him.' **Then we'll see what becomes of his dreams!"** *[11] One day, however, no one else was around when he went in to do his work. [12] She came and grabbed him by his cloak, demanding, "Come on, sleep with me!" Joseph tore himself away, but he left his cloak in her hand as he ran from the house.*
Genesis 37: 18-20; 39: 11-12 (NLT)

The misinterpretation of God's favor by others leads to jealousy and/or lust.
The love the brothers lacked from their father caused jealousy against Joseph. Their jealousy led them to want to "kill" the dream (God's favor). They saw Joseph as an offense to them, they felt *less than*, so they wanted to kill him/the dream. Favor comes from the Lord; therefore, comparisons are detrimental. One can never measure up to the favor of the Lord.

The love Mrs. Potiphar lacked from her husband caused her to lust for Joseph. Her lust led her to try to pervert God's favor. There are people who try to attach themselves to you because they want what you have. They can't explain why they want it, it's something they feel they must have. They lust for fleshly desires (physical pleasure, worldly treasures, status).
We should flee from these types of *relationships*, even if we need to leave something behind. Run, they are not of God! Running is safer than the hell we will find ourselves in. Understanding favor is not due to whom we are helps us with these challenges

because we will recognize it's all about the Lord. Anything or anyone, even our self-concept, not in alignment with that truth must be left behind.

The "dream" will come to pass regardless of the obstacles (ego, bondage, temptations, jealousy, lust, etc...) because it is of God. The timing of fruition remains to be seen.

"So then, it was not you who sent me here, but God..." Genesis 45: 8a

Misinterpreted favor of ourselves

² The Lord was with Joseph, so he succeeded in everything he did as he served in the home of his Egyptian master. ³ Potiphar noticed this and realized that the Lord was with Joseph, giving him success in everything he did. ⁴ This pleased Potiphar, so he soon made Joseph his personal attendant. He put him in charge of his entire household and everything he owned. ⁵ From the day Joseph was put in charge of his master's household and property, the Lord began to bless Potiphar's household for Joseph's sake. All his household affairs ran smoothly, and his crops and livestock flourished. ⁶ So Potiphar gave Joseph complete administrative responsibility over everything he owned. With Joseph there, he didn't worry about a thing— except what kind of food to eat!
Genesis 39: 2-6 (NLT)

We can be our own worst enemy when it comes to misinterpreting the favor of God. We can become full of ourselves and try to manipulate it into a self-serving dream. What happens when there are no attempts to manipulate, kill, or pervert the favor of the Lord? **It prospers.**

A righteous person with favor does not manipulate it, they submit to it. They are led by God and understand it all belongs to Him. Those around the individual make way for them because that's how God has ordained it and often end up blessed because of their presence. Look at Potiphar, the prison warden, and Pharaoh.

²³ The warden had no more worries, because Joseph took care of everything. The Lord was with him and caused everything he did to succeed. Genesis 39:23

[39] *Then Pharaoh said to Joseph, "Since God has revealed the meaning of the dreams to you, clearly no one else is as intelligent or wise as you are. [40] You will be in charge of my court, and all my people will take orders from you. Only I, sitting on my throne, will have a rank higher than yours."*

[41] Pharaoh said to Joseph, "I hereby put you in charge of the entire land of Egypt." Genesis 41:39-41

God's faithfulness

> *¹ After David was settled in his palace, he said to Nathan the prophet, "Here I am, living in a house of cedar, while the ark of the covenant of the LORD is under a tent."*
> *1 Chronicles 17: 1 (NIV)*

Cedars were considered the King of trees. They were a symbol of grandeur, might, loftiness and continuous expansion. David went from the fields and pastures to a palace of cedar. God is good and David knew it.

It had been many years between Samuel's anointing of David and his sitting in the palace, as King. There were many years and many trials, but God was faithful to His word. It is no wonder David entertained the thought of building a temple for the Lord (for the Ark of the Covenant to rest in). I'm sure if we settled long enough to think about how awesome God has been in our lives, we too would want to honor Him. I can only speak for myself, it doesn't matter whether I look at my life as a whole, season by season, or day by day, I want to honor God! Like David, I want to build something that will speak to His love, mercy and grace!

Sin

Solomon made an alliance with Pharaoh, the king of Egypt, and married one of his daughters.
1 Kings 3: 1a (NLT)

[1] *Now King Solomon loved many foreign women.* **Besides Pharaoh's daughter**, *he married women from Moab, Ammon, Edom, Sidon, and from among the Hittites.*
[2] *The Lord had clearly instructed the people of Israel, 'You must not marry them, because they will turn your hearts to their gods.'* **Yet Solomon** *insisted on loving them anyway.* [3] *He had 700 wives of royal birth and 300 concubines. And in fact, they did turn his heart away from the Lord.*
[4] *In Solomon's old age, they turned his heart to worship other gods instead of being completely faithful to the Lord his God, as his father, David, had been.*
1 Kings 11: 1-4 (NLT)

As I read, studied and prayed, I wondered how Solomon found himself in this position. God clearly put three words on my heart…"Not even one."

There are no exceptions to sin. Solomon found himself in this position, not because of his 700 wives and 300 concubines, but because of 1. Chapter 3 tells us that he made an alliance with Pharaoh and married 1 of his daughters. "Not even one."

This is the same Solomon who was wise enough to ask God for wisdom instead of riches and dominance over his enemies. He found favor with God and was given abundantly more than he asked for, *yet Solomon* opened the door to sin. He perverted his own favor! When we open the door to sin, it wears us down.

We can live in it and with it for so long that we become immune, and it (sin) becomes who we are. Solomon's heart was turned against God at an old age because he had years of practice (1 thousand women - documented). "Not even one."

It's easy to look at Solomon's story and shake our heads because his "numbers" are so high (1 thousand), but we've got "numbers", too. Remember, "Not even one." If we have 1, we have too many. If God says, "NO", it doesn't matter if it is one thing, one person, or one time; we are setting our hearts to turn against God. "Not even one."

Wise Counsel

*¹ After David was settled in his palace, he said to Nathan the prophet, "Here I am, living in a house of cedar, while the ark of the covenant of the LORD is under a tent." ² Nathan replied to David, "Whatever you have in mind, do it, for God is with you." ³ **But** that night the word of God came to Nathan, saying:⁴ "Go and tell my servant David, '**This is what the LORD says: You are not the one to build me a house to dwell in**.⁵ Nathan reported to David **all** the words of this entire revelation.*
1 Chronicles 17: 1-4, 15 (NIV)

Thank God for wise counsel, for it truly comes from Him! Wise counsel is able to listen to our intimate thoughts, encourage us, hear from God, and share the message…regardless of what our response may be. Wise counsel is more concerned with delivering the word of God righteously than stroking egos.

Nathan shows his faithfulness to God by sharing an answer that could cause David to feel rejected. Initially, Nathan encouraged David to do whatever his mind was telling him to do, because he knew he was a man after God's own heart. But later, God spoke *His* will to Nathan and he had to go back and tell the king God said, "No".

God has and will place people in your life to serve as wise counsel. Nathan shows us how we can be used, if we'll hear from God and deliver His messages. It's not enough to hear, we must be willing to share.

Trust

*24 I will answer them **before** they even call to me. While they are still talking about their needs, I will go ahead and answer their prayers!*
Isaiah 65: 24 (NLT)

I am overwhelmed with gratitude. I am thankful for the Lord hearing and answering my prayers *before* I pray them. How awesome for a Holy God to come so close to us - sinners saved by His grace.

I used to associate God's hearing and answering my prayers with receiving what I wanted. If I didn't receive what I was looking for, He must not have heard which explains my not receiving an answer. I felt I needed to pray a little harder and a little longer so He would hear and answer. The prayers and petitions were for His answering my way, not for Him to guide and direct. God wants to move us to a place where we just bring it to Him; no bells and whistles, no flips or cartwheels, just simply make our requests known to Him.

5 Trust in the LORD with all your heart and lean not on your own understanding; 6 in all your ways submit to him, and he will make your paths straight. Proverbs 3: 5-6

6 Do not be anxious about anything, but in every situation, by prayer and petition, with thanksgiving, present your requests to God. Philippians 4:6

Building / Rebuilding

¹ When the enemies of Judah and Benjamin heard that the exiles were building a temple for the LORD, the God of Israel, ² they came to Zerubbabel and to the heads of the families and said, "Let us help you build because, like you, we seek your God and have been sacrificing to him since the time of Esarhaddon king of Assyria, who brought us here." ³ But Zerubbabel, Joshua and the rest of the heads of the families of Israel answered, "You have no part with us in building a temple to our God. We alone will build it for the LORD, the God of Israel, as King Cyrus, the king of Persia, commanded us."

Ezra 4:1-3

Who are you building/rebuilding with and are you building/rebuilding with the same purpose?

Our enemies come with ill-intentions even if they frame it as "help". There is always opposition when building/rebuilding, so we must be careful whose help we accept. This sounds a bit unappreciative, but have you ever had a project sabotaged? Have you ever worked with a person or group who intentionally caused the project to fail? It's not a good feeling and I'd be willing to bet God was sending signs to alert you of the enemy in your midst. So, pray before accepting help. Not everyone desires to play a righteous part in your building/rebuilding.

A final thought…Building/rebuilding could be a work project, a relationship, a new job/position, a ministry, self-improvement goals, raising your child, etc…Not everyone deserves a part in your building/rebuilding.

We

*25 Arioch took Daniel to the king at once and said, "I have found **a man** among the exiles from Judah who can tell the king what his dream means." 26 The king asked **Daniel** (also called Belteshazzar), "Are you able to tell me what I saw in my dream and interpret it?"36 "This was the dream, and now **we** will interpret it to the king.*
Daniel 2: 25-26, 36 (NIV)

In verses 25 and 26, it appears only Daniel is taken to the king, so verse 36 caused me to ask, "Who is **we**?"

"We" accomplishes much more than "I" ever could. In fact, "I" often falls short, while "we" is always righteous. I need a "we attitude" like Daniel. So, what must I do to switch my I to we? Learn from Daniel…

- *8 But Daniel resolved not to defile himself… (Daniel 1:8)* He set himself apart.
- *Then Daniel praised the God of heaven 20 and said: "Praise be to the name of God for ever and ever; wisdom and power are his. (Daniel 2:19b-20)* He praised God.
- *23 I thank and praise you, God of my ancestors: **You** have given me wisdom and power, **you** have made known to me what we asked of you, **you** have made known to us the dream of the king." (Daniel 2: 23)* He thanked God and acknowledged where his power came from.
- *7 Daniel replied, "No wise man, enchanter, magician or diviner can explain to the king the mystery he has asked about, 28 but there is a God in heaven who reveals mysteries. (Daniel 2: 27-28)* He made it very clear that God was the One to reveal mysteries.
- Daniel sought God. *(Daniel 1-9)*

Under attack

*¹Darius decided it would be good to appoint 120 satraps to rule throughout the kingdom. ²Over these satraps were three officials. Daniel was one of these officials. The satraps were to report to these three officials so that the king wouldn't be cheated.³This man, Daniel, distinguished himself among the other officials and satraps **because** there was an extraordinary spirit in him. The king thought about putting him in charge of the whole kingdom. So the other officials and satraps tried to find something to accuse Daniel of in his duties for the kingdom. But they couldn't find anything wrong because he was trustworthy. No error or fault could be found. ⁵These men said, "We won't find anything to accuse this man, Daniel, **unless** we find it in his religious practices."*
Daniel 6: 1-5 (GW)

*¹³They replied, "Your Majesty, Daniel, **one of the captives** from Judah,...*
Daniel 6: 13 (GW)

Your attacks are bigger than you and most times are not personal. Not everyone will be happy about your elevation. They can't help it, there's something about you that rubs them the wrong way. In the case of Daniel, it was his background.

There didn't seem to be any problems until the king considered putting Daniel in charge of the whole kingdom. Keep in mind, these were all men of power, but for some reason "they" or "a group" felt Daniel didn't deserve to have as much power as the king was about to issue. "They" or "a group", as they are addressed beginning in verse 6, let the truth behind their conspiracy slip in verse 13. Your accusers will always reveal the real reason behind their attacks, if you stay quiet long enough. Remember, Daniel was a captive from Judah, a slave, who quickly rose as one of the king's favorites. They don't understand this elevation, but they feel it must not come to pass. They began to search for something to accuse Daniel of, but were left empty handed because Daniel was righteous. The only weapon they thought they had was Daniel's faith…it was a weapon - it is a weapon, but NOT for the enemy. What they thought they could use against him was the very thing that brought him through. (Take note of what your enemy tries to use against you…)

The attacks will come and they are bigger than us. It often comes down to someone thinking you shouldn't have what you have. Sad, but true, someone doesn't think you deserve your joy, your ministry, your spouse or relationship, your children, your home, your health, etc.. And the truth is we don't, *but God*!! "They" don't understand it's not ours; it's His. The world didn't give it and the world can't take it. They are confounded by the love God lavishes upon us.

We have to learn to work like Daniel worked; righteously. Glorify God in all we do, and when our accusers search to find something (and they will search), they will only find our relationship with God to bring charges against.
God has an answer for that, too…
"What can we say about all of this? If God is for us, who can be against us?" Romans 8: 31

What does your enemy see?

11 Then these men went as a group and found Daniel praying and asking God for help.
Daniel 6: 11 (NIV)

The attack is on and the enemy is watching…what does he see? The persecution is on and the enemy is watching…what does he see? Things are not going well…the enemy is watching…what does he see? The economy is bad, your job/position is in danger, you have illness in your body or in your family, life seems to be sucking the life out of you…the world is watching…what does the world see?

Prayerfully, they see us trusting God. And that looks like praying and asking God for help. We will be persecuted and under attack, but what separates us from the world should be our reaction. Somebody is watching and what they see will make a difference. It won't make a difference to the persecutor; the attack will continue because the enemy is focused on his mission (kill, steal, destroy). The difference will be how the next person "goes through". Someone, during their next trial, will seek God. To God be the glory and that is our mission!

The attack

¹⁰ Now when Daniel learned that the decree had been published, he went home to his upstairs room where the windows opened toward Jerusalem. Three times a day he got down on his knees and prayed, giving thanks to his God, **just as he had done before**.
Daniel 6: 10 (NIV)

The attack is in full swing! What do you do when you learn your attackers have their plan in place?

So many times we come under attack and disconnect from God. We become so stressed and fail to seek Him like we once did. Truth be told, we are angry because we are under attack. We wonder how righteousness merits an attack? True righteousness is from Jesus Christ who was persecuted for His righteousness…any more questions?? Maybe the attacks are less about us and more about God's glory. I heard it said, "If the enemy does not get in your way, perhaps it is a sign that you are on the same path."

So, what do you do when you learn your attackers have their plan in place?
Get on your knees and pray, give thanks to God.

Please note…until verse 21, you will not find Daniel uttering a word to anyone other than the One who could see him through.
Is this a hint at something else we should do?

Make your words count

21 Daniel answered, "May the king live forever! 22 My God sent his angel, and he shut the mouths of the lions. They have not hurt me, because I was found innocent in his sight. Nor have I ever done any wrong before you, Your Majesty."
Daniel 6: 21-22 (NIV)

He speaks, at last! What is the content of his words…Glory, honor and praises!

God spoke to me in such a way while studying about Daniel's reaction to his Lions' Den. He kept bringing to mind how Daniel went to Him and did not address his accusers, nor try to speak to the king. He could have…remember, he had "so distinguished himself" with the king. The king thought very highly of him, yet Daniel did not try to defend himself. It's one thing to be accused and keep quiet because the king does not know who you are or doesn't think very much of you, but when you **know** the king is on your side and you still "hold your peace"… That's God-given wisdom!

Daniel only speaks when he has something to say (read the entire book). When he speaks, it is with wisdom and integrity. Daniel was human. We don't know, perhaps he was unable to speak because he was angry at his accusers and confused by what was happening (Why didn't the king see through this plot? Why is God allowing this to happen?). As I said, we don't know and we don't know because Daniel had the wisdom to stay quiet.

Make a diligent effort to speak only when you have something to say. This challenge is not to imply that you don't think before you speak, but it's a discipline our world needs more of.

We don't always have to have an answer or "weigh in" on someone else's thoughts.

It's OK to listen and not share.

Lift your eyes

¹ I lift up my eyes to the mountains— where does my help come from? ² My help comes from the LORD, the Maker of heaven and earth.
Proverbs 18:21 (NIV)

²¹ Life and death are in the power of the tongue, and those who love it will eat its fruit.
Psalm 121: 1-2 (NIV)

When I lift my eyes to the mountains, I take them away from what is in front of me and focus them on what is ahead. I am looking past my situation to my solution. God is my solution and His promises are what I look to.

As long as I am seeking God, I can see beyond what's evident. Some of us are *Masters of the Evident*, but it doesn't take a genius to see what is in front of you. I don't need to focus on the chance that I may lose my job…I need to remember I've never seen the righteous forsaken nor his children begging for bread. I don't need to direct my thoughts on having made too many mistakes to move forward…I can do all things through Christ who strengthens me. I don't need to tell myself the relationship is dead…I need to dwell on the God who brings dead things back to life and calls into existence that which is not. In other words, speak life to yourself - encourage yourself.

New day

²This is the day the Lord has made.We will rejoice and be glad in it.
Psalm 118: 24 (NLT)

Yes, today is a new day! The alarm goes off and my eyes open as the computer of my mind logs on. The "To Do List" is on the screen and I form strategies for how I will accomplish each item. I have my morning devotions and my day begins. It's all very routine, but somewhere during the day there needs to be a time of rejoicing. To rejoice means to be glad; take delight. At what point am I glad or taking delight in this day? Do I spend my day grumbling, fretting about the next, and "living for the weekend"; only to get to the weekend and complain about how short it is?

Is there nothing to delight in? If the answer is "no", let's start all over again.

Today is a new day which means the past is behind and there are new opportunities. Rejoice!

You heard the alarm. Rejoice!

Your eyes opened and your mind is working. Rejoice!
New opportunities, hearing, seeing, thinking, etc… are all things we take advantage of until we don't have them anymore. Things don't always go the way we want them to, but go to sleep and, God willing, wake back up to a new beginning. There is someone who can counter each of those points because they choose to. Rejoicing is a choice and that is why the

Psalmist wrote, "We will…". They were making their choice known. Rejoice!

"True wisdom lies in gathering the precious things out of each day as it goes by." E. S. Bouton

2011

Empty ministry

*[2] "I know all the things you do. I have seen your hard work and your patient endurance. I know you don't tolerate evil people. You have examined the claims of those who say they are apostles but are not. You have discovered they are liars. [3] You have patiently suffered for me without quitting. [4] "**But I have this complaint against you. You don't love me or each other as you did at first!**
Revelation 2:2-4 (NLT)*

How do we find ourselves performing "empty ministry"?
If we don't love Christ and each other, our ministry is empty. Who are we working for? It looks good on the outside, e.g., Sunday School, Bible Study twice per week, Men's' Ministry, Women's Ministry, Children's Ministry, Ministry for the aged, Orphans Ministry, Widow/Widower Ministry, and the list goes on...**but** when we get to the core, there is no love. There's no love for Christ and there is no love for each other. So, again, how do we find ourselves in empty ministry? ROUTINES

Routines keep us on task and support us in getting the work done. Routines begin with good intentions, but the danger of routines is in the very nature of the concept, itself. They present a problem when we forget the reason <u>why</u> we are doing what we are doing.
A routine is a customary or regular course of procedure; commonplace tasks, chores, or duties as must be done regularly or at specified intervals; typical or everyday activity: *the routine of an office;* regular, unvarying, habitual, unimaginative, or rote procedure.

There is nothing regular, commonplace, typical, unimaginative or rote about Jesus Christ or the work of the Lord! When routines become the priority (our first love), we forget about Christ. There's no room for the Holy Spirit to have its way because it might throw us off schedule. We can't support this family because they don't meet the requirements for aide…there's no income and three children are hungry, but they don't meet the requirements? Where's the love for Christ and each other? Empty ministry…

The remedy: Get back to "why".
"…*Repent (change the inner man to meet God's will) and do the works you did previously [when first you knew the Lord],…*" Revelation 2: 5b (AMP)
2011

Lukewarm

[15] *"I know all the things you do, that you are neither hot nor cold. I wish that you were one or the other!*
[16] *But since you are like lukewarm water, neither hot nor cold, I will spit you out of my mouth!*
Revelation 3: 15-16 (NLT)

Lukewarm…I tried to think of a food or drink I enjoy at lukewarm temperature. I could not think of any food/beverage I would intentionally intake in a lukewarm state. Of course there are times it starts off at the perfect temperature and becomes room temperature. BUT, when I want a bowl of ice cream, my preference is not a melted bowl of ice cream. When I want a hot cup of tea, my preference is <u>not</u> a warm cup of tea. I don't reach for a lukewarm bottle of water on a hot and humid day. I am liable to spit it out because I want a cold bottle of water.

God wants people who love Him and will serve Him. He doesn't want a lukewarm son/daughter. To be lukewarm is to lack zeal, enthusiasm or show indifference. It brings to mind a word we used a lot when I was growing up, "wishy-washy". No one wanted to be around the "wishy-washy" person because you didn't know what to expect from one day to the next (sometimes from one minute to the next). Even if you didn't like it, you could respect the person that either liked you or did not. God wants to know are we for or against Him…a simple yes or no, not "maybe", "sort of", "somewhat", or "kind of". Our actions speak louder than words; God *knows all the things* we *do*.

What do our actions show God?

Admonishment

[But the Lord rebukes Jeremiah's impatience, saying]
If you have raced with men on foot and they have tired you
out, then how can you compete with horses?
Jeremiah 12: 5a (AMP)

I received a verbal admonishment from the Lord this morning. Our refrigerator went out and we had to call a representative to fix whatever the problem was. I was not happy, in fact, I was completely undone and irritated!

I said, "Really Lord…" and before I could complain, the Lord said,
"Really, Amy…really? A refrigerator? The refrigerator in the house I blessed you with? The refrigerator filled with food I've blessed you with? The refrigerator I have blessed you with the means to take care of? Really, Amy? Is the refrigerator going to stress you out? Are you really about to question Me about a refrigerator?"

Then, the Holy Spirit led me to pray for all the people on our prayer list. There were people who had lost loved ones, people who lost jobs, people without health care, people fighting to maintain their health care, people with sickness in their bodies and minds, people who have sick children…in other words, people who are COMPETING WITH HORSES while I'm tired out by a malfunctioning refrigerator.

I was so convicted and humbled as I prayed for my brothers and sisters. God was showing me the difference between racing with men and competing with horses. I'm thankful for the opportunity to repent from my complaining. I thank Him for the race that prepares me for the competition that He has already ordained a victory! All glory to God!

Misinterpretation of God's blessings

> [25] *When morning came, there was Leah! So Jacob said to Laban, "What is this you have done to me? I served you for Rachel, didn't I? Why have you deceived me?"*
> *Genesis 29: 25, 31-35 (NIV)*

[31] **When the LORD saw that Leah was not loved, he enabled her to conceive**, *but Rachel remained childless.* [32] *Leah became pregnant and gave birth to a son. She named him Reuben, for she said, "It is because the LORD has seen my misery. Surely my husband will love me now."*

[33] *She conceived again, and when she gave birth to a son she said, "Because the LORD heard that I am not loved, he gave me this one too." So she named him Simeon.*

[34] *Again she conceived, and when she gave birth to a son she said, "Now at last my husband will become attached to me, because I have borne him three sons." So he was named Levi.*

[35] **She conceived again, and when she gave birth to a son she said, "This time I will praise the LORD."** *So she named him Judah. Then she stopped having children.*

We can learn a lot from Leah's situation. The first is our misinterpretation of God's blessings.

God's blessings are never about us, but about His glory. Our blessings should draw us closer to God, not the world. Leah couldn't see it that way because she was unloved; first by her father, then by her husband. We know her father did not love her because he tricked a man into sleeping with her.

God blessed Leah with a child because He saw she was not loved, but she interpreted it as a way to get love. Four times she conceived and the first three times her focus was on man. Look at her process...first, she focused on getting love from Jacob, then with the next child she seemed to be grasping the blessing because she knew that the Lord saw/heard she was unloved, but the third time she was back to desiring the love of man. What I find interesting in her process is her "settling". Her self-esteem was low; she went from wanting Jacob to love her to just wanting him to be attached. This thought caused a long pause for me. If you have ever felt unloved or have settled for less than what God would have for you, you are probably pausing, too...

Only after she got so low that she was willing to "settle" for attachment instead of love did she grasp the blessing. With her fourth child/blessing, she praised the Lord! Her focus turned from the love of man to the love of God. Every good and perfect gift is from God...every good relationship, birth, job, talent...every breath we take deserves our attention to Him, not the world. Our attention; our praise should be to the Lord!

Unloved

[20] *So Jacob worked seven years to pay for Rachel. But his love for her was so strong that it seemed to him but a few days.*
[21] *Finally, the time came for him to marry her. "I have fulfilled my agreement," Jacob said to Laban. "Now give me my wife so I can marry her."*
[22] *So Laban invited everyone in the neighborhood and prepared a wedding feast.* [23] **But that night, when it was dark, Laban took Leah to Jacob**, *and he slept with her.* [24] *(Laban had given Leah a servant, Zilpah, to be her maid.)*
[25] *But when Jacob woke up in the morning—it was Leah! "What have you done to me?" Jacob raged at Laban. "I worked seven years for Rachel! Why have you tricked me?"*
Genesis 29: 20-25 (NLT)

Leah's situation shows us the importance of love beginning in the home of a child.

Laban's example as an unloving parent is extreme (unfortunately it does occur), but still illustrates what happens when children are raised in an unloving environment. If you strip away the disturbing circumstances, an unloving parent and an unloved child remain. Laban compromised his daughter, and as a result, she was constantly looking for love. God showed me that anytime a child lacks love, they are being compromised and sent on a journey of seeking love (usually from those who have no love for them).

I searched to read where Leah loved Jacob and couldn't find it. She told Rachel she stole her husband, but she didn't say she stole, "the love of her life". I tried more research and found either a focus on the "drama" or the romanticized "triangle". Bottom line, I couldn't find it in God's word and I believe she just wanted to feel loved. The world is an unloving place and when we send children into it without a firm understanding that someone loves them, we set them up for failed relationships. Someone, if not a parent, must show love.

Leah had a difficult time identifying love because she had not experienced it, which explains why she wanted it so bad from Jacob. It's a bad feeling not to receive love from ones who are *supposed* to love you…Pray for the unloved.

Quiet time

"Be still, and know that I am God!
Psalm 46: 10a (NLT)

I am a friend of God. He sticks closer than a brother, so I become concerned when I *can't* hear from Him. I'm always talking to or about Him, but realized I wasn't *hearing* anything. I started 'back-tracking', trying to figure out what I may have done to offend Him. Throughout the day, I listened carefully…nothing. When I lay down for bed, I listened…nothing. I woke up ready with a long list of things to do, then I heard it, a faint whisper, "be still".

I thought, "Cool, I'll run some errands and have some quiet time in between. I can study while I work out."

Not another whisper, but I knew I needed to stay home and be still. God clearly wanted me to spend some time with Him, but He will not beg for our time. If I had chosen to go, it would have been my choice to make, but at a cost. The house would not have gone up in flames, nor would lightning have shot down to strike me, *but* I would have missed out on precious time with my Lord.

"Whoever dwells in the shelter of the Most High will rest in the shadow of the Almighty." Psalm 91:1 (NIV)

Our mouths and our minds

⁸I [the Lord] will instruct you and teach you in the way you should go; I will counsel you with My eye upon you. ⁹Be not like the horse or the mule, which lack understanding, which must have their mouths held firm with bit and bridle, or else they will not come with you.
Psalm 32:8-9 (AMP)

Two things interfere with our understanding; our mouths and our minds - what we say and think.
If they are not controlled, we will have no understanding and no movement towards God. God tells us not to be like the horse or mule who only come when led by bit and bridle. A bit is placed in the mouth (tongue) and the bridle fits around the head (mind) to connect with the bit in order to control the animal.

God want us to be self-controlled. If we learn to control our thoughts and our tongues, we can hear more clearly from the Lord. When we hear clearly from God, we can receive His instruction, teaching, and counsel. Clarity from the Lord brings peace.

Do not walk, stand, or sit

*Blessed is the one who does not **walk** in step with the wicked*
*or **stand** in the way that sinners take*
*or **sit** in the company of mockers,...*
Psalm 1:1 (NIV)

Don't walk, stand, or sit...in other words; don't get comfortable in the dark.

We are in the world, NOT of the world; therefore, we do not function as the world does.
We don't take advice from wicked (evil or morally bad in principle or practice) men. They may be extremely intelligent, but wicked is wicked.
We don't spend our time standing with sinners. The amplified version defines "standing" as being passive and inactive. God wants us to be a light in darkness, not a dim bulb.
Lastly, and my favorite, don't lounge with mockers. This is my favorite because it can be easy to lounge in the company of a mocker, especially if you are too tired to move. A mocker is that person who attacks or treats everything with ridicule or contempt. You may not indulge in the attacks, their conversation may seem harmless, or the person may simply need to vent....**but** it is poisonous to your spirit. Check your attitude when you finish taking in all that "mocking"...I guarantee it is affected and not for the good.

"Blessed is the one who does not"...in other words; don't walk, stand, or sit in the dark and expect to be blessed.

Delight and meditate

¹ Oh, the joys of those who do not follow the advice of the wicked, or stand around with sinners, or join in with mockers. ² But they delight in the law of the Lord, meditating on it day and night.
Psalm 1: 1-2 (NLT)

Delight is a high degree of pleasure or enjoyment, joy. When I delight in the law of the Lord, I surround myself with Him or things/people with His likeness. In other words, I spend my time around those who can spiritually edify me and I them. Wise counsel is always nearby because I delight myself in those things of God, and wisdom comes from the Lord. I can stand and join in with those who are like-minded; set apart for His glory. There is no time or place for mocking because it does not bring glory to Him. There is no opportunity for the enemy to get a foothold because I am surrounded; inside and out (environment and mind) by Godliness.

Meditate is to engage in thought or contemplation, reflect. When I meditate on God day and night, it is all about Him. When a question or problem comes up, I seek a Godly answer or solution. I have an inner "What Would Jesus Do". I think on the goodness of God, so I can see that the day really wasn't so bad after all, and tomorrow will be better. I know that He is making a way because I reflect on the many ways He has already made. I wake up thinking about Him and go to sleep thinking about Him. I can call on His promises and know He is faithful.

In other words, today is going to be a good day.

Laugh at the enemy

¹ Why do the nations conspire and the peoples plot in vain?
² The kings of the earth rise up and the rulers band together
against the LORD and against his anointed, saying, ³ "Let us
break their chains and throw off their shackles."
*⁴ **The One enthroned in heaven laughs; the Lord***
***scoffs at them.** ⁵ He rebukes them in his anger and terrifies*
them in his wrath, saying, ⁶ "I have installed my king on Zion,
my holy mountain."
Psalm 2: 1-6 (NIV)

If God's response to the attempts of the enemy is to laugh, then
what should our response be? He is our Father and we are His
children, so if He laughs and has contempt for the plots of the
enemy, what should be our response?

I thought about children…"situations" arise and we tell them
not to worry about it. We tell them, "We'll take care of it ,"
and they trust us until the outcome is opposite their desires.
They don't always see what is best for them, so they begin to
keep things to themselves. They try to handle situations
themselves or double check on your progress of taking care of
matters. Is that what happens with us? We trust, we don't
receive "our" desired outcomes, so we become leery of leaving
"situations" in God's hands…

I wonder what would happen if we began to laugh at the
attempts of the enemy. What if we were so enraged by the
nerve of him to attack us that we began rebuking him
immediately?
What should my response be to the attempts, plots, attacks of
the enemy…Do I trust enough to laugh?

Striking and breaking

*Arise, LORD! Deliver me, my God! Strike all my enemies on
the jaw; break the teeth of the wicked.*
Psalm 3: 7 (NIV)

I must admit that I have always found, what I thought were,
David's "fits of anger" a little amusing and confusing, at the
same time. I was amused because I thought, "Boy, I'd like to
ask God to knock a few teeth out, but I know that's not loving."
I found it confusing because I wondered, "Those are not very
loving thoughts and requests. I do want God to deal with my
enemies, but can I really ask God for violent results?"

God caused me to think about David. David had been a
shepherd and he knew about wild animals. He was also a
writer; a poet, so he had the ability to capture our attention
with words. I read a few commentaries on this verse for
background information. Striking or slapping in the face/jaw
was a sign of scorn or contempt. (Trust me, it still is.) Breaking
or smashing the jaw and teeth of a wild animal would cause the
grip to be loosened on its prey; it would be helpless. He begins
this chapter talking about how many are his foes. David feels
surrounded by his enemies and likens them to wild animals.

Arise, Deliver, Strike, and *break* are David's call to God for action.
He wants God to have contempt for his enemies and render
them helpless. *Striking* and *breaking* illustrate the urgency of it
all!

Peaceful sleep

*ᴬIn peace I will **both** lie down and sleep, for You, Lord, alone
make me dwell in safety and confident trust.
Psalm 4: 8 (AMP)*

Have you ever thanked God for a peaceful night's sleep?
Unfortunately, peaceful sleep happens to be one of those things
we take for granted until we can't.
If you have ever lain in bed, eyes wide open, too burdened to
sleep, you can appreciate a peaceful night's sleep. I'd be willing
to bet you found yourself talking or crying out to God about
your desire for sleep.

The Lord *alone* is responsible for our peace, even when we are
sleep!

Laying and waiting

For I know the plans I have for you," declares the LORD, "plans to prosper you and not to harm you, plans to give you hope and a future."
Jeremiah 29:11

Laying my requests before the Lord, require me to transfer them from me to Him. They move from my hands to His. When I lay them before the Lord, I leave them with Him and never touch them again... Then, I wait expectantly; not anxiously, not impatiently, not in anguish, but **expectantly**.

For me, waiting expectantly on the Lord is waiting with anticipation. Reflect on a time you received a promise for something good. You already knew it was something you wanted; it was just a matter of receiving it. How did you wait? Waiting expectantly influences our attitude and mood. "I don't know when the house is going to come, but it's on the way. I don't know when my relationships will get better, but the change is in process. I don't know when I'm going to lose this weight, but I'm going to keep on eating right and exercising. I don't know when I'll be healed, but I'm thankful for each day. I don't know when my blessing is coming, but I'm next in line."

Lay your requests before the Lord, move out of the way, and watch Him work!

Unfailing love

*"Return, O Lord, and **rescue** me. **Save** me **because of your unfailing love**."*
Psalm 6: 4 (NLT)

"Not because of me, but **because of Your unfailing love**." Those five words cause me to pause and they cause me to put life into perspective.
Everything I am is because of His unfailing love. Everything I have is because of His unfailing love.

Focus on those words throughout your day. Because of His unfailing love..we opened our eyes this morning. "Unfailing love" is the mercy God shows us. When we think about God's mercy in our lives, we should be humbled; maybe even at a loss for words. I'll make it personal. When I think what God has brought me through in spite of my wretched behavior, I rejoice. When I think about what He shielded me from when I was too caught up in myself to love Him, my soul is stirred and I cry out, "Thank You!" Every day He allows new mercies, new opportunities to read, study and share His word *because* of His unfailing love. I am unworthy, yet because of His unfailing love I am rescued and saved.

When we begin to grasp the truth, we begin to look for ways to glorify Him because of His unfailing love.

Enemies

14See how that person conceives evil,
  is pregnant with harm, and gives birth to lies.
15He digs a pit and shovels it out. Then he falls into the hole
that he made for others. 16His mischief lands back on his own
head. His violence comes down on top of him.
Psalm 7: 14-16 (NLT)

The battle is not yours. The end of the story is already written
for the wicked; whatever evil they devise will come back on
them. Keep your hands off of "things" that don't belong to you
(i.e., battles, revenge, people). Remain prayerful for
righteousness. When we lay our spiritual weapons down and
take up our *worldly* weapons (e.g., gossip, schemes, etc...), we
cast ourselves into the role of the wicked.

How excellent, yet...

³ When I consider your heavens, the work of your fingers, the moon and the stars, which you have set in place, ⁴ what is mankind that you are mindful of them, human beings that you care for them? ⁵ You have made them a little lower than the angels and crowned them with glory and honor. ⁶ You made them rulers over the works of your hands; you put everything under their feet: ⁷all flocks and herds, and the animals of the wild, ⁸ the birds in the sky, and the fish in the sea, all that swim the paths of the seas.
Psalm 8: 3-8 (NIV)

Yet, we live and function as orphans…
Our Father in heaven, the Maker of the universe, the Alpha and the Omega has created us a "little lower than the angels", yet we squander our inheritance. We have bought into the lies of the enemy (we are less than conquerors and if the world is against us, we are defeated). We tremble and quake at every flaming arrow that comes our way, but God has blessed us with a shield of faith to extinguish each and every one. "Crowned" with "glory and honor", yet we refuse to take ownership of what is rightfully ours. He made us rulers over the works of His hands; everything under our feet…Why am I in debt? Why won't I be a good steward over what the Lord has blessed me with?

Step into your verse six reality!

Intimacy of praise

I will praise you, Lord, with all my heart;...
Psalm 9:1a (NLT)

As I think about praising God with all my heart, I realize how intimate praise is. Over this year, the Lord has blessed me to see various acts of praise. I reflect on the young lady who dances, the person who cooks for the choir, the school principal leading with integrity, the bell hop taking bags and giving his testimony, etc... I could go on and on because our praise is similar to our fingerprints; one of a kind. You don't have to understand mine, nor I yours because it belongs to the Lord.

Praise is why David danced, Jeremiah could not keep his mouth shut, Hezekiah received a life extension, and stones cry out!

David's honesty

¹Why are you so distant, Lord?
Why do you hide yourself in times of trouble?
¹⁴You have seen it; yes, you have taken note of trouble and
grief
  and placed them under your control.
    The victim entrusts himself to you.
You alone have been the helper of orphans.
Psalm 10: 1, 14 (GW)

Someone asked about my interest in David. They said I always find a way to study him / his life. It is simple to me, I appreciate his honest range of emotion. The Psalm begins with questioning God's distance during times of trouble, goes on about the wicked, and concludes with God's goodness. How often do you find yourself struggling with God's seemingly distant behavior when you are going through a season of struggle? We seem to feel unholy, if we admit that we are struggling with God's response or lack of response. Not David, just as he danced himself naked; his words dance naked before us.

Would a struggle be a struggle if we understood everything going on, had all the answers, and breezed through? Struggles are designed for us to work our way through them. The difference is how we go through. Psalms show us the difference between going alone and going with God. It is only when our relationship with God is strongly rooted that we can go from verse 1 to 14. Praise God for the writings of one who is after His own heart, so we may get a little closer to it.

Trust

> **¹ I trust in the Lord for protection.**
> **So why do you say to me**, *"Fly like a bird to the mountains
> for safety! ² The wicked are stringing their bows and fitting
> their arrows on the bowstrings. They shoot from the shadows at
> those whose hearts are right. ³ The foundations of law and
> order have collapsed.* **What can the righteous do?"**
> Psalm 11: 1-3 (NLT)

This reminds me of those who point out what "appears" to be
evident, who only see the negative, and are the bearers of all
things bad…They sit and watch the news or read the newspaper
and discourage you from any forward movement. They
pronounce doom and gloom on the living. Tell them of an
illness and before you begin your, "…but Jesus…" praise, they
have chosen the font for your obituary. They tell you to take
flight without realizing that all you need to do is "look to the
hills". The saddest part of all is these words are sometimes
spoken by "believers".

When trouble seems to be all around and the attack is on, we
can find peace in the remaining verses of Psalm 11.

Psalm 11: 4- 7 (NLT)
⁴ But the Lord is in his holy Temple; the Lord still rules from heaven.
  He watches everyone closely,examining every person on earth.
⁵ The Lord examines both the righteous and the wicked.
    He hates those who love violence.
⁶ He will rain down blazing coals and burning sulfur on the wicked,
    punishing them with scorching winds.
⁷ For the righteous Lord loves justice.
    The virtuous will see his face.

Serving

[30] Simon's mother-in-law was in bed, sick with a fever, and they told Jesus about her at once. [31] He went to her, took her by the hand, and raised her up. The fever left her, and she served them.
Mark 1: 30-31 (CEB)

Praise God for those who go to Jesus and tell Him about us!
Thank you Jesus for coming to us, touching us, and raising us up from whatever lowly state You finds us in.
Our life changes in such a significant way from the time our Lord enters it, that our response should be to honor and serve Him.

Everybody is looking for you

³⁶*And Simon [Peter] and those who were with him followed Him [pursuing Him eagerly and hunting Him out],*
   ³⁷*And they found Him and said to Him,* **Everybody is looking for You**.
Mark 1: 36-37 (AMP)

I watch, read, or hear the news and come away with the same conclusion, "Everybody is looking for You."
I listen to conversations and/or stories at work and social situations and think, "Everybody is looking for You."
I observe life around me and see, "Everybody is looking for You."

Like Simon Peter and the other followers, once you become acquainted with the awesomeness of Jesus, you know He is the answer. You listen to people and hear Simon Peter's words in the background. You hear of or see violence and abuse and your heart breaks thinking of the truth. Our struggles with addiction, depression, low self-esteem and fear are rooted within these five words. Everybody is looking for Jesus!

Immediately

⁴²**Immediately**, *his skin disease went away, and he was clean.*
Mark 1: 42 (GW)

²⁹ **Immediately** *the bleeding stopped, and she could feel in her body that she had been healed of her terrible condition.*
⁴² *And the girl, who was twelve years old,* **immediately** *stood up and walked around! They were overwhelmed and totally amazed.*
Mark 5: 29, 42 (NLT)

I was reading a passage in the book of Mark and came across the word "immediately". The word seemed to jump off the page at me and I thought to myself, "I could use some *immediately* in my life." I would be willing to bet that I am not the only one. The Lord prompted me to read through Mark for "immediately", so I did.

I searched my Bible which is an earlier NIV and found the word quite a few times; each time strategically placed. It caused me to ask, "What preceded the word *immediately*?" I studied more and noted it was preceded by either extreme faith or extreme doubt. Furthermore, the circumstances were usually extreme (e.g., leprosy, paralysis, disease, death, etc…). I shook my head and decided that maybe I don't really want "some immediately in my life". Perhaps I'll just continue on with faith and trust in the Lord's time line.

God helped me to see that we often want *immediately* without the trials that precede it. We see what seems to be an immediate blessing in the lives of others without knowing the pain or suffering that may have led to it. "Immediately" refers to the timing of Jesus' response, in that moment, not the time/length of the issue.

Paralyzed

> [3]Then they came, **bringing a paralytic to Him**, who had
> been picked up and was being carried by four men. [4]And when
> they could not get him to a place in front of Jesus because of
> the throng, they dug through the roof above Him; and when
> they had scooped out an opening, they let down the [thickly
> padded] quilt or mat upon which the paralyzed man lay. [5]And
> when Jesus saw their faith [their confidence in God through
> Him], He said to the paralyzed man, Son, your sins are
> forgiven [you] and put away [that is, the penalty is remitted,
> the sense of guilt removed, and **you are made upright
> and in right standing with God**].
> Mark 2: 3-5 (AMP)

Have you ever gone to Jesus for one thing and He blessed you
with another? Perhaps not what you wanted, but what you
needed…

The man was paralyzed; there was no doubt he could not move
on his own and was in need of a healing…but what kind of a
healing? Only the Lord and this man knew his sins, and I am
convinced this man came to Jesus because of his physical
paralysis, but Jesus saw another type of paralysis within. The
AMP's break down of "your sins are forgiven and put away"
confirmed what God was blessing me with.

This man, who was *paralyzed*, was made *UPRIGHT* and in *right
STANDING* with God when his sins were removed. God is
much more concerned with our spiritual afflictions than our
physical. He didn't (at first) give the man what he came for, but
gave him what he needed. We are blessed that our God is one
of priority!

What do you see?

*15 Later Jesus was having dinner at Levi's house. Many tax collectors and "sinners" were eating with him and his disciples. They were part of the large crowd following Jesus. 16 Some teachers of the law who were Pharisees were there. **They saw** Jesus eating with "sinners" and tax collectors. So they asked his disciples, "Why does he eat with tax collectors and 'sinners'?" 17 Jesus heard that. So he said to them, "Those who are healthy don't need a doctor. Sick people do. I have not come to get those who think they are right with God to follow me. I have come to get sinners to follow me."*
Mark 2: 15-17 (NIV)

What we *see*, can be interesting.
The Pharisees saw Jesus eating with tax collectors and "sinners". Our earlier NLT refers to them as "notorious" sinners while other translations/versions refer to them as "wicked", "stained", "scum", and "disreputable". Wow! They must have been quite a crew for everyone to have known them as sinners (it's rough when your sins are out in the open), yet they were obviously also known for following Jesus (v15)… It reads, "They were part of the large crowd following Jesus."

The Pharisees saw Jesus eating with scum, notorious, wicked, stained, disreputable sinners because they were there…What were they doing at Levi's house with this group of "sinners"? Were they invited, then surprised that Jesus was there? Were they invited because they fell into that same group, but were surprised when Jesus showed up and afraid that their true identity would be revealed? We do like to "see" the sins of others, but find ourselves in the same places.

It's interesting what we see when we look at others, but not at ourselves…I love Jesus' response in verse 17.

It is dangerous to be sick and not know it.

Think about what you are thinking about

> [8]*Finally, brothers and sisters, keep your thoughts on whatever is right or deserves praise: things that are true, honorable, fair, pure, acceptable, or commendable.*
> *Philippians 4: 8 (GW)*

> [27] *She had heard about Jesus, so she came up behind him through the crowd and touched his robe.* [28] *For she thought to herself, "If I can just touch his robe, I will be healed."* [29] *Immediately the bleeding stopped, and she could feel in her body that she had been healed of her terrible condition.*
> *Mark 5: 27-29 (NLT)*

I can't control what pops into my mind, but I can control what I do with it. I can entertain it or I can rebuke it. I can dwell on negative thoughts and ruin my day, OR I can replace the negative with Philippians 4: 8. "Keep your thoughts…" lets me know that I have choices in what I **keep** in my mind.

The woman in Mark 5: 25-26 had a lot to think about. She could have thought about suffering, being at the end of her bank account, alienation (Lev. 15:25-30), rejection, being taken advantage of, etc… BUT she heard about Jesus and chose to think on something that deserved praise, something true, pure, honorable, etc…Some translations/versions use "She said…" instead of "she thought…"; either way, it was in her mind. What she entertained during her personal time was important.

What we entertain in our minds gives us power. When she touched Jesus' garment, He felt power go out of Him! She touched his garment because she thought she would be healed and she was. Make an effort to think about what you are thinking about.

My lack of faith

And **because of their unbelief**, he couldn't do any
miracles among them **except** to place his hands on a few sick
people and heal them.
Mark 6:5 (NLT)

I have always read Mark 6 and shook my head at the unbelief in
His hometown. I had moved onto another passage when
"**except**" in verse 5 caught my eye.
"…he couldn't do any miracles among them **except** to place his
hands on a few sick people and heal them." It hit me - Jesus still
blesses us in our unbelief. He didn't leave them with nothing,
He just couldn't give all He had because they didn't have enough
faith. Many questions began to fill my mind.

How much does my lack of faith hinder my blessings? Jesus has
blessed me, but what if I'm receiving the minimal blessing
because my faith is minimal? What if there was something
beyond what I received?

Because of her faith, the woman in chapter 5 received healing,
peace, and freedom from her suffering. She received beyond
healing. The paralytic in chapter 2 received forgiveness of his
sins AND he was healed. He received beyond.

I believe Jesus goes beyond for faith that goes beyond (e.g., the
woman pressed through all that would hinder her and the
paralytic was in relationship with some brothers willing to tear
the roof off to get to Jesus).

Jesus is present

⁴⁷When evening came, the boat was in the middle of the sea, and he was alone on the land. ⁴⁸Jesus saw that they were in a lot of trouble as they rowed, because they were going against the wind. Between three and six o'clock in the morning, he came to them. He was walking on the sea. He wanted to pass by them. ⁴⁹When they saw him walking on the sea, they thought, "It's a ghost!" and they began to scream. ⁵⁰All of them saw him and were terrified. Immediately, he said, "Calm down! It's me. Don't be afraid!"
Mark 6: 47-49 (GW)

There are a few lessons to learn in these verses.

Jesus is always watching; even during our struggles.
It was evening when Jesus saw them and He went to them in the early morning. He had to have had His eye on them in order to go out to them.

Struggle comes with discipleship.
Jesus saw them struggling in the evening, yet did not go near them until between three and six o'clock in the morning. He had planned to allow them their struggle, but they screamed in fear when He passed by. (How many storms did the disciples find themselves in? How many times were they in the midst of some type of struggle?)

Jesus is present, but sometimes we can't identify Him.
Jesus watched from land, walked out on the water, and walked by the boat. They thought He was a ghost. The disciples were consumed with their struggle and functioning in so much fear that they could not identify Jesus.

Jesus will allow struggle, but not fear.
He was willing to pass by them while they were struggling, but revealed Himself when they were terrified! He does not want us operating in fear. God has not given us a spirit of fear, but one of power, love, and a sound mind. He told them, "Calm down!" (sound mind), "It's me." (love), "Don't be afraid!" (power).

Again

¹ One day as Jesus was standing by the Lake of Gennesaret, the people were crowding around him and listening to the word of God. ² He saw at the water's edge two boats, left there by the fishermen, who were washing their nets. ³ He got into one of the boats, the one belonging to Simon, and asked him to put out a little from shore. Then he sat down and taught the people from the boat. ⁴ When he had finished speaking, he said to Simon, "Put out into deep water, and let down the nets for a catch." ⁵ Simon answered, "Master, we've worked hard all night and haven't caught anything. But because you say so, I will let down the nets." ⁶ When they had done so, they caught such a large number of fish that their nets began to break. ⁷ So they signaled their partners in the other boat to come and help them, and they came and filled both boats so full that they began to sink.
Luke 5: 1-7 (NIV)

I did some reading about fishing with nets and came across this quote,
"Many times after several hours and hundreds of throws with a cast net, many fishermen are asking themselves 'is this worth the effort?'"

Can you relate? What are you doing or trying to figure out that leaves you asking, "Is this worth the effort?" It could be a personal goal, a project at work, getting your finances in order, a relationship, etc…Perhaps we need to follow Jesus' directions to Simon; go into the deep and let your net down. In other words, "try again". It had to be extremely frustrating for Simon to work hard with no results and then be directed to do what he had probably already done. Simon had been using a boat which means he had been fishing in deeper waters, **but this time**, he would have Jesus on board. Not only did he have the "Master" on board, but he followed what he had been told to do (of course after stating what he'd already done, which unfortunately I have this same tendency). The results were an abundance he couldn't carry alone.

Maybe the missing piece to the puzzle continuing to frustrate us is making sure Jesus is on board, we are listening to Him, and doing what He tells us…even if it appears to be what we've already done.

Jesus prayed

12 It was at this time that He went off to the mountain to pray, and He spent the whole night in prayer to God. 13 And when day came, He called His disciples to Him and chose twelve of them, whom He also named as apostles:
Luke 6: 12-13 (NASB)

I've been reading about Jesus choosing the *twelve* since I was a little girl and was tempted to skip reading it again. After all, I've been reading it or it's been read to me for at least a good 40 years now, what could be new?

Just to be clear, the "He" mentioned above is Jesus Christ, Son of God, our Savior. So, if **He** spent the night in prayer before making a decision, what would make us think we could make a sound choice or decision without spending time in prayer?

Mercy

*32 "If you love those who love you, what credit is that to you?
Even sinners love those who love them. 33 And if you do good to
those who are good to you, what credit is that to you? Even
sinners do that. 34 And if you lend to those from whom you
expect repayment, what credit is that to you? Even sinners lend
to sinners, expecting to be repaid in full. 35 But love your
enemies, do good to them, and lend to them without expecting
to get anything back. Then your reward will be great, and you
will be children of the Most High, because he is kind to the
ungrateful and wicked. 36 Be merciful, just as your Father is
merciful.*
Luke 6:32-36 (NIV)

It's so hard for us to give the very thing God renews for us on a
daily basis.
Morning by morning, new mercies I see…yet, cross me and
find out what I will extend. Sad isn't it, but I'm only human,
right? If you share the sentiment that our flesh is an excuse for
disobedience, then you will want to reread the last part of verse
35. You may see a familiar face. I did…I saw my
ungratefulness and wickedness covered by God's love. That is
mercy. In spite of my "enemy-like" behavior (disobedience,
anger, doubt, fear, etc…), He wakes me with *new* mercies each
and every morning!

We should embrace the opportunity to be merciful.

Storms

7 During the days of Jesus' life on earth, he offered up prayers and petitions with fervent cries and tears to the one who could save him from death, and he was heard because of his reverent submission.
Hebrews 5:7 (NIV)

It is amazing how the "storms" of life cause us to stop and think. There are storms that cause us to pause, and then there are storms that cause us to stop.

I have never seen the hand of God moving like I have during our vacation. "Storms" are a good metaphor for the troubles we face in life. The rain we witnessed while away was extraordinary. It rained from Sunday to Thursday. It would let up here and there, but for the most part it was pretty consistent. The thing was, you never knew when a great wind would come and torrential rains would fall. You didn't know where you would be and umbrellas provided limited protection. We watched the beautiful grounds flood and smelled the fumes of poor irrigation. We were walking to dinner and the power went out...nothing but darkness. The only thing you could be sure of was that God was in control. If you EVER lose perspective of Whose Hands you are in...go through a storm...a storm that makes you "stop". I'm sure if you have been through or are going through a storm of life, you can relate to the untimeliness of rain and winds, the inefficiency of umbrellas, the flooding and stench of improper irrigation (the flushing and washing out of anything), and not knowing when you will find yourself stumbling in the dark.

The good news is when you know whose Hands you are in. Knowing you are in God's hands is what makes you STOP and let go of all the "things" you think you have within your grasp and hold to His unchanging hand. Storms will also cause you to reexamine your walk…knowing there is potential for a hurricane to hit a place that does not have a secure foundation will cause you to make a decision about whether you are cold, hot or lukewarm. The cold don't care enough to cry out, the lukewarm don't take the threat seriously enough to move beyond themselves to cry, but the "hot"…they have intensely passionate (fervent) cries and tears with deeply respectful (reverent) submission. God showed me those cries, tears, and submissions are not about "save me", but Lord let me and my house be with You whichever way this storm falls.

I was watching a news report and heard a government official say, 'We are trying to help people as much as possible before the storm and the high winds hit, but when the storm hits, there's nothing more we can do until it passes.' I thought "Amen".

Offer up prayers and petitions with fervor and reverent submission for those who face the natural and spiritual storms of life. Pray for God's mercy. Pray for God's people to truly know they are in His hands and He is in control.

Offended

*"A person's wisdom yields patience; it is to one's glory to
overlook an offense."*
Proverbs 19:11 (NIV)

Sister Soinso didn't speak to me at church. In fact, she looked
past me as though I wasn't there. Brother Uknowwho left my
name off the ministry's distribution list and Rev. Minister didn't
acknowledge my contribution to Friday's fish fry. As a result, I
am offended. I am angry and my feelings are hurt!

The reason they did not acknowledge me is simple. I am not
their number one priority, and the reason I am so upset is
because I am my own number one priority. My being angry or
offended serves one purpose and that is to add fuel to the
enemy's fire. He couldn't be more pleased when we become
self-consumed and spiteful toward one another. When I am
offended, my prayers are self-serving. I pray for patience and
for God to hold my tongue. I pray for God to strengthen me
while in my offender's presence, but when do I pray for the
person? When do I pray for God to meet them at their point of
need? There is a need.

People are struggling. We see them in church serving,
ministering, singing and greeting us with a smile, but we don't
see what happens when they go home. They cry, they sleep,
they don't sleep, or they do a little of each. Is it any wonder
they don't see you, they forget your name or don't acknowledge
your contributions (even though we did it for the glory of
God…)?
Please, stop being offended and start being prayerful. God has
called us to encourage and build each other up.

Armed

24 "When an evil spirit leaves a person, it goes into the desert, searching for rest. But when it finds none, it says, 'I will return to the person I came from.' 25 So it returns and finds that its former home is all swept and in order. 26 Then the spirit finds seven other spirits more evil than itself, and they all enter the person and live there. And so that person is worse off than before."
Luke 11: 24-26 (NLT)

All cleaned up, but unarmed…
The house is swept and in order, but more is needed. God is constantly directing us to, "Guard your…", "…put on the full armor…", or "…clothes yourselves with…". Being clean, but unarmed is a playground for the enemy. The evil spirit leaves, roams around looking for another life to disrupt and comes back with a vengeance. It brings seven others and someone is "worse off than before".

The enemy is coming back strong, but we have weapons; spiritual weapons! We have to be clean *and* armed.

10 A final word: Be strong in the Lord and in his mighty power. 11 Put on all of God's armor so that you will be able to stand firm against all strategies of the devil. 12 For we are not fighting against flesh-and-blood enemies, but against evil rulers and authorities of the unseen world, against mighty powers in this dark world, and against evil spirits in the heavenly places. 13 Therefore, put on every piece of God's armor so you will be able to resist the enemy in the time of evil. Then after the battle you will still be standing firm. 14 Stand your ground, putting on the belt of truth and the body

*armor of God's righteousness. 15 For shoes, put on the peace
that comes from the Good News so that you will be fully
prepared. 16 In addition to all of these, hold up the shield of
faith to stop the fiery arrows of the devil. 17 Put on salvation
as your helmet, and take the sword of the Spirit, which is the
word of God.
Ephesians 6:10-17 (NLT)*

CROWN

the top part of the tree, branches grow from it and support the leaves, each crowns differs according to the role it plays

Go

17 He is before all things, and in him all things hold together.
Colossians 1: 17 (NIV)

My will versus God's will is a challenge when I see nothing before me, yet continue to hear, "Go..." Like a child, I keep walking and looking up to my Father to make sure He is still with me and sometimes checking to make sure that He is sure. I keep holding on and shaking my head saying, "OK, I know you know best, but did you see/hear what I just saw/heard? I'm just asking..."

I marked this verse and revisited it frequently. Each time...nothing. I read it, knowing it was for my present journey, but could not gain clarity. I repeated and read the words several times throughout the day. Revelation finally came. Regardless of what this present journey or any other looks like in the natural, Christ is before it and IN Him, it all holds together. Peace comes after wrestling with the word of God. I can continue to *go* confidently.

God gives the increase

2 The Lord said to Gideon, "You have too many warriors with you. If I let all of you fight the Midianites, the Israelites will boast to me that they saved themselves by their own strength. 3 Therefore, tell the people, 'Whoever is timid or afraid may leave this mountain and go home.'" So 22,000 of them went home, leaving only 10,000 who were willing to fight. Judges 7:2-3, 7, 12 (NLT)

Doors close, people leave, finances dry up…It's disheartening to watch your help / support leave in the face of a battle or huge undertaking, but you can trust the decrease. We serve a God who is more than able. We can stand on His promise that if He is with us, none can be against us.

God had already told Gideon he was the one to deliver the Israelites out of the hands of the Midianites, so he only needed to be obedient and trust. God cut Gideon's army from 32,000 to 300…God, not satan. 300 against an enemy so numerous that their camels could no more be counted than the sand on the seashore. Why? The decrease was needed so "the people" would not think the victory came from their own strength; not Gideon, but the people. Gideon knew it was God because he was no warrior, yet was called to lead an army. God needs us and those around us to be sure where our help comes from.

So, as uncomfortable as it is, trust the decrease.

God willing

13 *Look here, you who say, "Today or tomorrow we are going to a certain town and will stay there a year. We will do business there and make a profit." 14 How do you know what your life will be like tomorrow? Your life is like the morning fog—it's here a little while, then it's gone. 15 What you ought to say is, "If the Lord wants us to, we will live and do this or that." 16 Otherwise you are boasting about your own plans, and all such boasting is evil. 17 Remember, it is sin to know what you ought to do and then not do it.*
James 4: 13-17 (NLT)

I have a friend who always says, "God willing…" before any plans she shares. I've heard her say it many times, but for some reason, the other day I was convicted. I am guilty and I confess that I have a very bad habit of reserving my "God willing…" for, what I tend to consider, big things… "God willing, I'll get the job. God willing, I'll see you at next year's Family Reunion." BUT, I'll share my plans for the week as if they are written in stone. "This week, I will run to store on Tuesday. I'll go to the meeting on Wednesday and I'm getting my hair done on Saturday."

It is quite boastful and rooted in thinking that I handle the small stuff and God handles the big stuff. It's like I'm delegating and allowing Him to take part in my life. How kind of me…It is a sin and I must begin to speak with my mouth what I say I know in my heart. The truth is if I really know and believe this truth, I should have no problem speaking / confessing His power in all areas of my life (big and small). It is a confession…if God is not willing, there are no completed plans.

Your core

13 *For I can do everything through Christ, who gives me strength.*
Philippians 4:13 (NLT)

A few years ago, I made a move at the gym and the result was sciatica. If you have never suffered from sciatic pain, God bless you! And if you have, God bless you! I chalked it up to turning 40 and "the old bod not being what it used to be". After resting, I began physical therapy and shared my thoughts on how the injury occurred with the therapist. In my mind, I had done nothing wrong other than make a wrong move. It had to be age. After a series of strength assessments, the therapist explained the injury was not due to age, but my weak core. He explained that many injuries occur because we do not take the time to strengthen our core. It was not due to age, simply put, I had a weak core. I went to physical therapy for a few weeks and was left with a series of exercises to do regularly to strengthen my core.

So, how strong is your core? We can do all things "through" Christ, who gives me strength. Are you doing *through* Christ or on your own? Just like our bodies...I can work out at the gym seven days per week and twice on Sunday, but if my core is weak...I can sustain an injury at any time. If my core, my strength through Christ, is weak then I am setting myself up for spiritual injuries.

Hands off

God wants us to be still and KNOW that He is God. We show we KNOW by taking our hands off (whatever your hands are on...take them off!).

God made this very clear to me in such a simple way...
My workout routine is to take my iPod which is filled with music to feed my spirit and be fed as I do my cardio. I climb on the machine, turn on my iPod and go to my self-created Play-list. As I begin moving, I pull up my Play-list; hit "shuffle" and the machine shuffles the songs to play in a random order so I can be free to work out. Understand, I made the Play-list to consist of songs that minister to me for this season I am in. Yet, I listen for the first song, and then push the forward arrow for another song of my choosing. I do this regularly; it's my routine.

On this particular day, the first song was, "You've been so faithful" by Eddie James. I listened, and prepared to push the forward arrow for what I wanted to hear next. The next song was, "Before I die" by Kirk Franklin. I listened, and then prepared to push the forward arrow for what I wanted to hear next. The next song was another good one and after it finished, before I could touch the iPod...God clearly said, "Take your hands off." He told me if I would just take my hands off, I would be free to receive. He wanted to minister to me. I became teary-eyed because I realized how "hands on" I really am. I set up my Play-list to hear songs to minister to me, then I push "shuffle" to hear them in random order...then I control what I was supposedly leaving alone. I get so busy trying to do the business of God that I end up trying to do God's business…

I took my hands off and received so much that I was overwhelmed. Not only did God pour into my spirit, He allowed me a great workout. Our Lord is awesome! If we take our hands off, He will fill our every need. He blessed my spiritual and physical being.

> 5 *Trust in the Lord with all your heart; do not depend on your own understanding.* 6 *Seek his will in all you do, and he will show you which path to take.* 7 *Don't be impressed with your own wisdom. Instead, fear the Lord and turn away from evil.* 8 *Then you will have healing for your body and strength for your bones.*
> *Proverbs 3: 5-8*
> (2011)

Leadership

I have been studying and learning about good leadership in preparation for a new position at work. I recognize God's word as the blueprint for any success, so that has been my guide. All summer, I have had a book on my Kindle titled, "Lead Like Jesus". It's my husband's book, but I have had access to it and not read it. For some reason, I've not been interested in opening it until the other day.. I began reading it and thought to myself, "Wow! Why didn't you begin this book earlier?" Before I could begin fooling myself with lies, the truth came out.

I didn't start earlier because I was interested in *tips* on how to lead like Jesus, but not actually leading like He did. I was still struggling with the assignment God had given me, so I was no where near thinking about leading like Him. Until you accept the assignment, you can't wrap your mind around your duty. We want leadership to be about getting along and being in charge, which is unrealistic if you want to lead like Jesus Christ. Leading like Jesus is accolades one week and a cross the next, on the team one week, Judas kiss the next. We can't lead in our power or strength.

I have finally accepted the assignment (you can take the position and not necessarily accept the assignment). I am a work in

progress and moving past only wanting tips from the Lord. With tips, I still get to work in my own strength. I can be unforgiving and say, "Oops, I didn't realize I was supposed to forgive the person who undermined my project…" I realize opposition will come with serving God's people, but more importantly, I am learning that healing, truth, peace, and victory override opposition. Praise God, I also realize Jesus already did the hard work; He only wants me to lead like Him, not be Him. Glory to God and thank you Jesus!!!
Be the leader God is calling you to be…

23 Then Jesus said to them all, "If anyone wants to follow Me, he must give up himself and his own desires. He must take up his cross everyday and follow Me. 24 If anyone wants to keep his own life safe, he must lose it. If anyone gives up his life because of Me, he will save it. 25 For what does a man have if he gets all the world and loses or gives up his life? Luke 9: 23-25

Praying for spiritual leaders

5 So Peter was held in prison. But the church kept praying to God for him. 11 As Peter began to see what was happening, he said to himself, "Now I am sure the Lord has sent His angel and has taken me out of the hands of Herod. He has taken me also from all the things the Jews wanted to do to me." 12 After thinking about all this, he went to Mary's house. She was the mother of John Mark. Many Christians were gathered there praying.
Acts 12: 5, 11-12 (NLV)

For the last few years, I have watched our spiritual leaders publicly come under attack and be defeated by the enemy. I'm tired because the victory over the enemy has already been won, but we're living defeated.

I read an article about a pastor found dead and it broke my heart. I can remember hearing his testimony of how God delivered him from sin. I had read and heard many stories about him since hearing that testimony, and he was in a lot of pain. You could see it on his face, hear it in the stories, read it in the article, and know it by the final report of his death. I was troubled as I read the article because the writer went on to say that this man's inner circle and congregation failed him by not holding him accountable. True as this may be (I don't know one way or the other), I don't think it is a complete truth. I agree we are to hold one another accountable, but I think accountability without prayer is judgment. What troubles me about the words I read and the stories I hear is there is no mention of our accountability as God's people to lift and cover our leaders in prayer.

The young man and many of us are like the house cleaned of the evil spirit, but not guarded. The evil spirit comes back with seven others and creates havoc! When we don't cover our leaders in prayer, we leave them as naked prey for the enemy who is roaming; seeking to steal, kill and destroy. These are men and women of God...flesh and blood, which means they have weaknesses; just like us. The difference is they are in the spotlight whether in a mega-church or a corner church. Every time they stand before God's people, the enemy is angry. he knows our struggles and what he doesn't attack with temptation, he inflicts with sickness, financial burdens, and/or family woes. Our job is to guard our leaders in prayer, so even when they are groping in darkness, they may find light.

It's time to put down our stones and pray for our spiritual leaders. Gossip and judgment are tools of the enemy to keep us from lifting and covering in prayer. The verses above refer to Peter being jailed for preaching the word of God and the people were praying for him. In other words, he found himself in bondage for preaching God's word...Many of our spiritual leaders are in bondage because satan is angry for their anointing to preach/teach the word of God. What were the people doing? Praying. What happened? He was set free. I encourage you to choose one day of the week to focus your prayers on the spiritual leaders of your church and of our world.

Trust

41 Jesus said to her, "Martha, Martha, you are worried and troubled about many things. 42 Only a few things are important, even just one.
Luke 10: 41-42a (NLV)

I confess, I have had a "Martha Mind" and I am exhausted.

It's official, I am worn out from trying to figure things out. I am always trying to make sense of things; therefore, I weigh options, explore scenarios, and attempt to reason. My mind has become so cluttered that I can't hear answers from God. I've left no room for Him. I've asked questions and answered them before I hear a whisper from Him.

I know it sounds like the iPod shuffle again and it is! Since the Lord told me to take my hands "off", it's been like scales falling from my eyes. On the surface, my intentions have been good. I want to be in God's will, but below the surface (once again), I've been trying to shape God's will around my own. Bottom line, all those "things" I've been trying to figure out are really "things" I have been worried about. Worry does not come from the Lord; it is a lack of faith and trust. Yet, God is faithful and has shown me where my mind needs to be and where my energy/focus needs to be.

Where does my mind need to be? Colossians 3:2
Think about the things of heaven, not the things of earth.

Where does my energy/focus need to be? Matthew 6:33
Seek the Kingdom of God above all else, and live righteously, and he will give you everything you need.

The more time I spend thinking on earthly things, the less time I have to seek the Kingdom of God. The less time I spend seeking the Kingdom of God, the more unmet needs I will have.

> *"Be still, and know that I am God!..."*
> *Psalm 46:10a*

Lies of the enemy

10 But Moses pleaded with the Lord, "O Lord, I'm not very good with words. I never have been, and I'm not now, even though you have spoken to me. I get tongue-tied, and my words get tangled."
Exodus 4:10

15 "But Lord," Gideon replied, "how can I rescue Israel? My clan is the weakest in the whole tribe of Manasseh, and I am the least in my entire family!"
Judges 6:15

5 Then I said, "It's all over! I am doomed, for I am a sinful man. I have filthy lips, and I live among a people with filthy lips...
Isaiah 6:5

6 "O Sovereign Lord," I said, "I can't speak for you! I'm too young!"
Jeremiah 1:6

11 "Who told you that you were naked?" the Lord God asked.
Genesis 3:11

What have you been told about yourself that you have accepted as truth? Was it that you were slow, weak, too young, damaged, or not good enough? Who told you that you were …?

Someone planted a seed (or seeds) in us long ago, either knowingly or unknowingly. The enemy rushed in and got a foothold into our minds and hearts. We accepted it as truth and it served or is serving as a hindrance to the purpose God has for our lives. What the enemy doesn't want us to know or acknowledge is we serve a God who specializes in the flawed. Why else would He send His beautiful, perfect son to die for sin-stained us? God sees past our weaknesses and calls us to be warriors, leaders, teachers, preachers, and prophets!

The next time you look in the mirror or identify yourself as *anything less than a child of God*, ask, "Who told you that you were …?" The devil is the father of lies.

14 I praise you because I am fearfully and wonderfully made; your works are wonderful, I know that full well.
Psalm 139:14

Be mindful of the seeds *you* plant.

Praise and worship

25 Around midnight Paul and Silas were praying and singing hymns to God, and the other prisoners were listening. 26 Suddenly, there was a massive earthquake, and the prison was shaken to its foundations. All the doors immediately flew open, and the chains of every prisoner fell off! 27 The jailer woke up to see the prison doors wide open. He assumed the prisoners had escaped, so he drew his sword to kill himself. 28 But Paul shouted to him, "Stop! Don't kill yourself! We are all here!" 29 The jailer called for lights and ran to the dungeon and fell down trembling before Paul and Silas. 30 Then he brought them out and asked, "Sirs, what must I do to be saved?" Acts 16: 25-30 (NLT)

I find myself in awe when I consider how Paul and Silas' praise and worship loosened, not only their chains, but those of *all* the prisoners. It was midnight; they were praising and singing after being dragged, stripped, beaten, and severely flogged! Their wounds weren't close to being healed, in fact, they hadn't been cleaned, yet they were singing and praising. It's not the angelic or melodious voices, but praise through the pain that frees us. True praise and worship has the power to loosen your chains AND the chains of those around you.

More powerful…our chains are not loosened for our benefit. God loosens our chains for others. Paul and Silas were "free" to leave. They could've picked up their clothing and limped home, but instead they chose to stay back for the one who was commanded to keep watch over their imprisonment! The result, the salvation of an entire family! This makes me wonder what we are doing with our freedom…are we reaching back, reaching out, or moving along?

Praise God for freedom and give Him glory by being a blessing to others.
2011

Gratefulness

15 One day some parents brought their little children to Jesus so he could touch and bless them. But when the disciples saw this, they scolded the parents for bothering him. 16 Then Jesus called for the children and said to the disciples, "Let the children come to me. Don't stop them! For the Kingdom of God belongs to those who are like these children. 17 I tell you the truth, anyone who doesn't receive the Kingdom of God like a child will never enter it."
Luke 18:15-17 (NLT)

When was the last time you had child-like excitement about Jesus? When was the last time you sat full of wonder and admiration? When was the last time you were care-free because of Him?
Have you become so accustomed to His goodness that you take Him for granted or are you simply so sophisticated in your knowledge of Him that you are no longer moved one way or the other? Perhaps you are stale; you've sat on the shelf so long and lost your flavor…Maybe you are tired; tired of waiting for Him to come through on those promises made so long ago…Are you burdened…burdened by taking care of everything yourself?

Children (those not spoiled by their gifts) are always happy to receive gifts! It is not until we *grow up* that we learn to be ungrateful and question the value of the gifts we have received, or pout because the gift is *late*. It's a learned behavior when children think they are "owed" something. They are usually thrilled to receive a gift! Young children rely on the one in charge for everything. They believe everything they are told and trust that the one in charge is truly in charge. They take all of their questions and concerns to the one in charge. They are without a care and free to enjoy the gifts they are given. They don't take themselves seriously.

We would do well to open our eyes to the awesome and undeserved gifts we receive daily: life, new mercies, forgiveness upon repentance, full coverage and protection, joy, peace, wisdom and healing to name a few! Let us not forget family, friends, laughter, health, shelter, clothing, food, etc…These gifts, when recognized, keep us fresh. Jesus loves when we are child-like because He is then free to mold us into the person He died for us to be.

Leadership

I treasure peace and quiet. At work, I have been longing for a quiet place to regroup, gather my thoughts, and put on my armor so I can push down my flesh to be filled with His spirit. My work station does not provide peace or quiet, in fact, I am positioned for constant interruption. It is a room inside of a room, surrounded by windows. Colleagues look into the room and enter with questions and/or requests. Groups meet regularly in that space, so if I am not part of the group, I must leave. I am in a hub, but I have come to realize God is doing a new thing and it is taking me out of my comfort zone. I am a "close your door" type of gal. It's my way of shutting out and shutting down. Well, God informed me that I can't pick and choose who (and when) I serve, if I am truly serving Him. Leadership means being accessible to the needs of others.

God knows His child and knows I need a place of refuge (not hiding) in order to function righteously. I have been praying to find a place with minimal interruptions, so I can go pray and jump back into the rush of things. God is faithful! A colleague and I found ourselves organizing a closet and I remarked, "We spend so much time in here; this should be our place to pray." We looked at each other and knew we'd found our spot!

Sometimes, we are so busy mumbling in our frustrations that we can be standing in an answered prayer and miss it! The Lord is my shepherd; I shall not want!

Praise

*7Turn all your anxiety over to God because he cares for you.
8Keep your mind clear, and be alert. Your opponent the devil
is prowling around like a roaring lion as he looks for someone
to devour.*
1 Peter 5:7-8 (GW)

I sat in the bed with a sore throat and body aches. I decided to
retrace my steps in order to figure out how the germs got in. I
can usually identify the "culprit act" (wearing no hat, a sick
colleague or family member, etc...). As I started from Sunday
and mentally walked through each day, I found the truth. God
had blessed me with an awesome week! I had experienced God
in many different ways during the week and not that sneaky
devil wanted to stifle my praise with sickness.

I made a decision that no matter how bad I felt, I would
continue to praise God. I would not allow this minor setback to
define my week with the Lord. It's easy to lose sight of
blessings because the enemy is hell bent on stealing our joy.
Great things happen and here he comes to send a cloud or a
shadow...sickness in the family, struggling child, bouncing
checks, and dying car engines. What *monkey wrench* has he
thrown into your day to make you lose sight of your blessings?

If the enemy can throw us into a whirlwind of self-centeredness
or self-pity, we will never sing praises to our God. We'll never
get a clear message of what God wants us to do because we are
meditating on things we have no control over (verse 7). As a
result, we are devoured.

Knowing the voice of God

*The gatekeeper opens the gate for him, and the sheep listen to
his voice. He calls his own sheep by name and leads them out.
4 When he has brought out all his own, he goes on ahead of
them, and his sheep follow him because they know his voice.
John 10: 3-4, 27 (NIV)*

*27 My sheep listen to my voice; I know them, and they follow
me.*

*Now the serpent was more crafty than any of the wild animals
the LORD God had made. He said to the woman, "Did God
really say, 'You must not eat from any tree in the garden'?"
Genesis 3:1 (NIV)*

There is something so comforting about the voice of God.
Whether He is setting you straight, encouraging you, or just
whispering a word; it is the most awesome sound. I believe
God is always speaking. We either can't hear because we have
too much noise around us or we are unable to distinguish His
voice. As I study God's word and reflect on hearing from God,
I realize there are two ways I am *always* sure of His voice.

The first, He tells me things I would never tell myself and
instructs me to do things I cannot do on my own.

The second way I have learned to distinguish God's voice is very
soon after I hear it, the enemy attempts to steal it.
It's the voice of doubt. You *know* you heard the promise, but
you question, "Did God really say…?" This voice focuses on
everything in the natural; everything your human eye can see
set against the direction or the promise. The enemy's purpose

is to cloud your thinking and leave you in a state of confusion, so you begin to reason that it was not from God.

The best way to hear and distinguish the voice of God is to spend so much time with Him that it is unmistakable.

Stand firm

17 When Pharaoh let the people go, God did not lead them on the road through the Philistine country, though that was shorter. For God said, "If they face war, they might change their minds and return to Egypt." 18 So God led the people around by the desert road toward the Red Sea. The Israelites went up out of Egypt ready for battle.
Exodus 13:17-18 (NIV)

13 Therefore put on the full armor of God, so that when the day of evil comes, you may be able to stand your ground, and after you have done everything, to stand.
Ephesians 6: 13 (NIV)

Put it on and stand. Put it on and stand firm! Why? The Israelites show us you can be armed for battle, but not ready for war. So, put it on and stand firm. It's amazing, that standing firm is all we are required to do, besides putting on the armor. I keep repeating it to myself because I get zealous. I put the armor on and start flexing my sword and making warrior moves…that's a sure way to get burned by one of those flaming arrows. Why? Because I'm moving in my own strength. I am confident in MY abilities (don't do it).

God needs to direct our steps because there are some battles, that although we may be armed, we are not ready. The Israelites went up out of Egypt ready for battle, yet God took them the long way around because He knew their true nature. We become zealous and in denial. God knows there are some things we cannot handle because we would rather run back to slavery and bondage than fight. It would be a shame to do all those warrior moves and end up running with your tail between your legs.

It takes discipline to stand. Stand firm today at work, at home, or at school when you are challenged to speak words you should not or participate in an act you have no business being a part of. Stand firm when folks try to draw you into a negative conversation with unwholesome talk. Stand firm when it seems easier to cheat than study. What we have to remember is standing firm doesn't mean inaction, it is God in action. When we are standing firm, we are trusting God with all of our hearts and leaning not to our own understanding. We are acknowledging Him in all our ways, so He can make our paths straight.

Put it on and stand.

Fear

18 There is no fear in love. But perfect love drives out fear, because fear has to do with punishment. The one who fears is not made perfect in love.
1 John 4: 18 (NIV)

I was heavy most of the day and could not pinpoint why.

God spoke to me about fear and love through verse 18. He showed me the fear around me and the love I needed to show. I felt badly for those "poor souls" functioning in fear, but thankful that God had taken the time to show me their dilemma…Did I mention that I was heavy most of the day and could not pinpoint why?

Later that evening, I was at church and the minister touched on fear. It was as if a video of my day was playing on the screen of my mind. I was so "in tune" with the fear everyone else had that I couldn't see the spirit of fear weighing on me (we ought not think too highly of ourselves). God showed me my heaviness was due to my fears, which were causing me to *not* show love. I wasn't mean or rude, but I was protecting myself. I had my guard up. Love removes self and doesn't seek to protect it. It trusts and hopes; therefore, always thinking the best. I'm so thankful for God showing me "my poor soul"! I have to go forward in God's perfect love and then, and only then, can I show love.

4 Love is patient, love is kind. It does not envy, it does not boast, it is not proud.
5 It does not dishonor others, it is not self-seeking, it is not easily angered, it keeps no record of wrongs.

6 Love does not delight in evil but rejoices with the truth.
7 It always protects, always trusts, always hopes, always perseveres.
8 Love never fails.
1 Corinthians 13: 4-8a

I can't be light until I learn to walk in the Light. Less of me; more of Him!

Pressing

12 Not that I have already obtained all this, or have already arrived at my goal, but I press on to take hold of that for which Christ Jesus took hold of me. 13 Brothers and sisters, I do not consider myself yet to have taken hold of it. But one thing I do: Forgetting what is behind and straining toward what is ahead, 14 I press on toward the goal to win the prize for which God has called me heavenward in Christ Jesus.
Philippians 3: 12-14 (NIV)

I don't believe it is a coincidence that Paul used words like press and straining. It requires effort to move forward without holding on to the past or revisiting the "old". Life's disappointments have a way of turning us just enough to look at what is behind us. It's amazing; our present disappointments and pain can blur our vision to a point that the past doesn't look so bad. When fatigued from pressing and straining forward, the past never looks like the hell it was. Somehow, it looks comfortable and functional.

Disappointed by the travel arrangements and menu, the Israelites longed for the "good old days" of slavery. Are you kidding me…longing for slavery, missing bondage? But were they much different than us when moving forward is not the party we thought it would be?
We decide to stop smoking and gain ten pounds…we think, at least when I smoked my weight was manageable. I might as well go back to smoking.
We decide to sever ties with a long-time friend and our weekends are filled with Lifetime Movies, reality shows and popcorn…we think, at least I wasn't lonely and bored. I might as well make the call.

We try so hard not to smoke that we replace the cigarettes with chips, brownies, and Snickers? We try not to miss our previous relationship and end up living vicariously through the dysfunctional relationships of others? It's not moving forward that presents the problem; it's how we choose to spend our time while moving forward.

Paul didn't look behind because he was too focused on his God-given purpose. He didn't have time (nor did he make time) to relive the past. We need to strain toward something new from the Lord. Even if we aren't sure of our purpose, we can strain toward seeking God for answers. 9/25/2011

Reminder that we are dependent

⁵ ...apart from me you can do nothing.
John 15:5 (NIV)

Today is a new day! This verse presents a promise that will shape every second of our day and week. If I choose to embrace this in my heart and mind, I will be productive. Nothing will be too hard, too stressful, or too much to ask because I can do ALL things through Christ who strengthens me, but I can do nothing apart from Him. The promise is simply stated and powerfully true. Apart from God is nothing, and in God is everything.

Technology and modern inventions allow me the ability to create reminders of God's promises, yet sometimes I have to go old school and write them on my hand. I liken these visual reminders to Proverbs 7:1-3.

Sin

7 Then the eyes of both of them were opened, and they realized they were naked; so they sewed fig leaves together and made coverings for themselves.8 Then the man and his wife heard the sound of the LORD God as he was walking in the garden in the cool of the day, and they hid from the LORD God among the trees of the garden. 9 But the LORD God called to the man, "Where are you?"
Genesis 3: 7-9 (NIV)

We must hear the voice of God ask, "Where are you?"
Isn't that a reality check? God knows where we are, but calls us to be accountable. He knows we are knee-deep in sin, but WE have to face it and know it before we can grow from it. The more we deny it, the further we move from intimacy with God.

Adam and Eve shared such an intimate relationship with God that they felt the effects of their sin immediately. Opened eyes and nakedness are the conviction we feel in our spirits when we sin. Sin leaves us stripped and we attempt to "cover" ourselves. We hide, lie, and blame in efforts to cover up the shame, but we are ill-equipped to re-cover from sin on our own. We can sing praises because God has covered us from the beginning of time!

21 The LORD God made garments of skin for Adam and his wife and clothed them.

God's will

"…Yet not as I will, but as you will."
Matthew 26: 39b (TNIV)

What new thing is God trying to do?
What "old" thing, way, or mind set are you clutching?

God wants to do something new to and/or through you. Before we get excited and think, "shiny new", we must accept that God's "new" is sometimes less than shiny. This *new* is not necessarily the one we have been praying about, but the one we need. This *new* has the potential to take us out of our comfort zone, so we don't move in our own strength. We move closer to the One who is able to sustain us.

God's "new" can look a little like this:
a Savior born to an unwed, teenage virgin impregnated by the Holy Spirit
the King or Kings born in a manger and wrapped in rags
Righteousness congregating with unrighteousness
a Messiah washing feet as a servant
Sinless crucified for the sinful

God's *new* is setting aside how things have always been done or what feels most comfortable in order to embrace His will be done.

Love

*12 Because of the increase of wickedness, the love of most will
grow cold,…*
Matthew 24: 12 (TNIV)

Love never fails.
1 Corinthians 13: 8a (TNIV)

We live in a world of increased wickedness. Look around,
watch the news and read the newspaper; you may feel
hopeless. There's death, destruction, deceit, and
disillusionment. Even what is considered entertainment is
dipped in debauchery. Love can grow cold because we feel
helpless, which is exactly what the enemy wants. he wants us to
feel tired, defeated, and abandoned. he likes when we question
God's presence and leave an opening for doubt to flood our
souls. When doubt moves in we allow our weapon to grow
cold. Love is the greatest weapon. For all that 1 Corinthians
13 teaches about love, let us not forget or look past the fact that
- love never fails. Those three words are a promise we have to
believe and know because the world is tough. We have to
remind ourselves and each other that even in the increase of
wickedness, love never fails.

*And so we know and rely on the love God has for us. God is
love.*
Whoever lives in love lives in God, and God in them.
1 John 4: 16 (TNIV)

Comforting others

3 Praise be to the God and Father of our Lord Jesus Christ, the Father of compassion and the God of all comfort, 4 who comforts us in all our troubles, so that we can comfort those in any trouble with the comfort we ourselves receive from God. 2 Corinthians 1: 3-4 (TNIV)

God comforts us so we can comfort others, SO we must rely on Him to direct our efforts. We need to look to the Lord for words to speak and actions to take; which includes silence. I'm not sure that silence is a comfort we've mastered giving. I haven't; I still get a little uncomfortable in silence. I'm a "fix it" type of person, so in silence I begin searching for words to say. Have you ever shared words of comfort (scriptural or otherwise) and the person looked at you blankly? God's word is always on time, it's our delivery that is lacking. Sometimes God is directing us to listen and other times, He wants us to extend our arms and give a hug. I think of how God comforts me…there are times I clearly hear God speak words of encouragement and there are other times I feel His calming spirit all around me.

Apart from God, I can do nothing; not even comfort a brother or sister in need. So, the next time I find myself in a position to comfort another, I will wait on the Lord.

Live in love, not fear

₁ It is for freedom that Christ has set us free. Stand firm, then, and do not let yourselves be burdened again by a yoke of slavery.
Galatians 5:1 (TNIV)

₁₇ Now the Lord is the Spirit, and where the Spirit of the Lord is, there is freedom.
2 Corinthians 3:17 (TNIV)

Freedom allows us to live in love, not fear. Fear is what keeps us enslaved. We are afraid of our past, so we can't move forward. We are afraid of being "found out", so we cover up. We are afraid of consequences, so we hide. We are afraid of rejection, so we withhold love.
We don't live! We duck and dodge the truth; whether it is the truth of our past, our present or the truth of our future.

When we have the Spirit of the Lord, we have all the truth we need. We live knowing the truth of our past; the debt has been paid and there is absolutely nothing we did or could do to earn it. The truth of our future is we have eternal life, and let us not forget the truth of our present; We Are Free! Our past, present, and future are summed up in one verse.

For God so loved the world that he gave his one and only Son, that whoever believes in him shall not perish but have eternal life.
John 3:16

Love casts out fear

26 *Jesus answered, "It is the one to whom I will give this piece of bread when I have dipped it in the dish." Then, dipping the piece of bread, he gave it to Judas, the son of Simon Iscariot.* 27 *As soon as Judas took the bread, Satan entered into him.*

So Jesus told him, "What you are about to do, do quickly." John 13: 26-27 (TNIV)

Lately, God has been revealing a great deal to me about fear. I guess more specifically; my fears. I was asked, "What would you do, if you knew someone you love was going to betray you?"

I was taken aback and wondered "who", but my response came quickly. I said I would keep them close enough to keep an eye on them and I would begin cutting the strings of attachment now, so it would not hurt as much in the end.

The next question..."Is that what Jesus did?"

Of course we know the answer is "no", but it made me think deeply about my response and Jesus' response to Judas. My response is a perfect example of fear. My goal is to protect myself; my emotions. I will change the dynamic of our relationship, so you can't hurt me.

Jesus shows love and is love. Imagine knowing someone in your inner circle was going to betray you...not just someone, but you know their name and their actions are going to kill you. Yet, He loved Judas. Judas was not just one of the disciples; he was one of the "twelve". Jesus looked at him on a regular basis knowing he was a great link to the anguish He would experience for our sake. Yet, we never read where Jesus mistreated Judas or withheld love. I believe Jesus was so focused on God's glory that He saw beyond Judas. He loved Judas in spite of, and that, I cannot comprehend.

I read years ago that fear is the opposite of love. It was a nice thought, but I didn't get it. As my relationship with God grows more intimate, I see and experience love. I have learned there is no way love and fear can function in the same vessel. Jesus is always rebuking fear; He will not tolerate it. It is opposite Him.

The perils of love are great. Do you show love or do you hold back? Do you hold onto the deceit of others or do you move on in love? Do you dwell on the pain or do you walk in your purpose? Do you fight those who would seek to destroy you or do you leave it in the hands of your Father and say to them, "What you are about to do. Do quickly."
We are not Jesus, but we have received the love of Jesus; even in our betrayals.

...so that Christ may dwell in your hearts through faith. And I pray that you, being rooted and established in love, 18 may have power, together with all the Lord's people, to grasp how wide and long and high and deep is the love of Christ, 19 and to know this love that surpasses knowledge—that you may be filled to the measure of all the fullness of God.
Ephesians 3: 17-19

God's will

42 He went away a second time and prayed, "My Father, if it is not possible for this cup to be taken away unless I drink it, may your will be done."
Matthew 26: 42 (TNIV)

53 Do you suppose that I cannot appeal to My Father, and He will immediately provide Me with more than twelve legions [more than 80,000] of angels?
54 How, then, are the Scriptures to be fulfilled that say this must happen?"
Matthew 26: 53 (AMP)

Whose will be done? Can you tell the difference?
Does this verse not give clear evidence to those questioning if Father and Son are one?
Is this what the Lord desires from us…that we become so intimate with Him that our will cannot be separate from His?

Five words take the sacrifice to another level for me; "and He will immediately provide…" In verse 42, Jesus is agonizing to be in alignment with God's will; three times He prays to get in line with God. Now, in verse 53 we read that all Jesus would need to do is send up a word and God would *immediately* provide 80,000 angels (not the sweet blushing cherubs with flutes, but warrior angels equipped for battle), yet He does not. So, the cup could have been taken away, but because of love - He chose us.
Incomprehensible!

…so that Christ may dwell in your hearts through faith. And I pray that you, being rooted and established in love, 18 may

have power, together with all the Lord's people, to grasp how wide and long and high and deep is the love of Christ, 19 and to know this love that surpasses knowledge—that you may be filled to the measure of all the fullness of God.
Ephesians 3: 17-19

A familiar enemy

*Eliab, David's oldest brother, heard David talking to the men.
Then Eliab became angry with David. "Why did you come
here," he asked him, "and with whom did you leave those few
sheep in the wilderness? I know how overconfident and
headstrong you are. You came here just to see the battle." Saul
responded to David, "You can't fight this Philistine. You're
just a boy, but he's been a warrior since he was your age."
When the Philistine got a good look at David, he despised
him. After all, David was a young man with a healthy
complexion and good looks.*
1 Samuel 17: 28, 33, 42 (GW)

These three verses remind of me of three types of enemies we
can have. The first enemy is familiar, but we don't consider
them (or it) an enemy. The second is an enemy that has not yet
been identified, and the third we know very well as our enemy.
Eliab represents the first type of enemy.

He is the familiar opposition we don't consider an enemy, but
make no mistake, he is. Eliab was David's oldest brother and
most times the older sibling looks out for the younger, but I
imagine it hard to look out for one with the ability to kill lions
and bears. He probably always saw David's anointing and stood
in opposition to him, but being passed by for the anointing was
offensive. His being denied the anointing led to envy which led
to confirmation of his "enemy" status. Eliab used his position of
familiarity to belittle David's shepherding and to attempt to
slander him by labeling him as overconfident and headstrong.
You know those family members and/or old friends who always
want to remind you that they knew you "when".

This enemy wants to place their limitations on us. We must deal with that enemy, no matter how close in relationship, just as David did Eliab…"turn away".

> He then turned away to someone else and brought up the same matter, and the men answered him as before.
> 1 Samuel 17: 30

Enemies: Unapparent and apparent

> *Eliab, David's oldest brother, heard David talking to the men. Then Eliab became angry with David. "Why did you come here," he asked him, "and with whom did you leave those few sheep in the wilderness? I know how overconfident and headstrong you are. You came here just to see the battle." Saul responded to David, "You can't fight this Philistine. You're just a boy, but he's been a warrior since he was your age." When the Philistine got a good look at David, he despised him. After all, David was a young man with a healthy complexion and good looks.*
> *1 Samuel 17: 28, 33, 42 (GW)*

The Lord has positioned you to slay a giant and not only do you have your "Goliath" to contend with, but you have the preconceived notions and insecurities of others to deal with. Someone is angry with your presence, someone is judging you by what they "think" you bring to the situation, and someone despises you and you don't know why. Yet, none of that matters because God has assigned you to kill that giant. The sooner we embrace that truth, the sooner we can put our Goliath out of its misery. We can stop worrying about what they said and why they said it because Eliab, Saul, and Goliath each have issues with you that are grounded in their own shortcomings.

Eliab is angry because David's presence diminishes his. Eliab has been there, but done nothing and now here comes his little brother to show him up. That's not David's purpose, but Eliab knows David is capable. David's confidence and strength intimidates him.
Saul is the king, but he's been standing and listening to Goliath insult the Lord; just standing and listening… He can't see past

his fear of Goliath, so he tells David that he is too young and Goliath has been a warrior since he was a boy. If he, a grown man, is frozen in fear, there's no way this boy can fight. After all, Saul is the king.

Lastly, we have Goliath...he despises David because he is everything he is not or perhaps he is everything he once was. He looked David up and down, and he too was intimidated. The difference between Eliab and Goliath was one knew the ability and the other underestimated the ability. (The other difference is - one is David's "brother" and the other his "known" enemy, not that we can see much of a difference, but that's a story by itself.)

As you slay your giants this week, don't allow Eliab, Saul, or Goliath to cast a shadow of doubt on your ability to do what God has assigned you to do. They serve no purpose for God, only the enemy, so keep your stride in the Lord.

Praise

If my lungs expand with His praise, then breathing and praising are simultaneous for me!

The expanding of the lungs is the inhalation process of breathing; in other words, it is necessary for normal breathing. It is interesting The Message (MSG) translation chooses to use "expand with his praise" rather than "expand and contract", which is what healthy lungs do. The purpose of the lungs is to bring oxygen into the body (the lungs expand) and to remove carbon dioxide (the lungs contract). Oxygen is the gas that provides energy and carbon dioxide is a waste product.

When my lungs expand with His praise…

I receive inspiration; the process of "inhalation" is also called INSPIRATION.

I receive energy.

I have the ability to release some "waste product" in my life.

I don't have to think about praising God, I just do it. Unless you are unhealthy, you don't have to think about breathing; you just do it. Unless you are spiritually unhealthy, you don't have to think about praising; you just do it!

Jesus' love

Now a man named Lazarus was sick. He was from Bethany, the village of Mary and her sister Martha. 2 (This Mary, whose brother Lazarus now lay sick, was the same one who poured perfume on the Lord and wiped his feet with her hair.) 3 So the sisters sent word to Jesus, "Lord, the one you love is sick." 4 When he heard this, Jesus said, "This sickness will not end in death. No, it is for God's glory so that God's Son may be glorified through it. 5 Now Jesus loved Martha and her sister and Lazarus. 6 So when he heard that Lazarus was sick, he stayed where he was two more days. . .
John 11: 1-6 (NIV)

5 So although Jesus loved Martha, Mary, and Lazarus, 6 he stayed where he was for the next two days. (NLT)

5 Jesus loved Martha and her sister and Lazarus. 6 Yet when he received the news that Lazarus was sick, he stayed where he was for two more days. (GNT)

"He stayed where he was…"
He wasn't detained by indifference, illness, prison, nor transportation; He stayed. He purposely and intentionally stayed where He was for two more days. He loved them, all three, Mary, Martha, and Lazarus, but Jesus stayed where He was. The sisters called for Jesus in their time of need and although He loved them, He stayed where he was…two more days.

I'm not sure what I find more alarming…the fact He chose to stay or my "understanding" of the NIV wording. It reads to me as though He stayed because He loved them and if that's true, then…

His love is incomprehensible.

His love is not defined by response time.

His love is not defined by distance.

His love has the ability to shake our faith.

Waiting

5 Now Jesus loved Martha and her sister and Lazarus.
6 So when he heard that Lazarus was sick, he stayed where he was two more days, 7 and then he said to his disciples, "Let us go back to Judea." 8 "But Rabbi," they said, "a short while ago the Jews there tried to stone you, and yet you are going back?"
John 11: 5-8 (NIV)

The intentionality of stating Jesus loved this family is brilliant! Everything that follows reflects God's love for us.

We are puzzled by Jesus' decision to wait two days before going to see about Lazarus; His making us wait. How can He love us, know we are in pain and in need of His present-presence, yet "stay back"? We ask ourselves and Him those questions, but we should be equally inquisitive of the next two verses. Jesus put himself in danger to bring Lazarus back to life. We can't explain why He would knowingly put Himself in danger, especially since He could have just spoken his healing like He did for the official's son. We can't explain why He would go through beatings and death for us when He could've called a legion of angels to save Him? So many questions…

We question Jesus because we question His love. We question His love because it is incomprehensible (1 Corinthians 13). Jesus is love and His every action is love…understand, agree, like it, or not; it's all love.

Following Jesus

7 and then he said to his disciples, "Let us go back to Judea."
8 "But Rabbi," they said, "a short while ago the Jews there tried
to stone you, and yet you are going back?" 9 Jesus answered,
"Are there not twelve hours of daylight? Anyone who walks in
the daytime will not stumble, for they see by this world's light.
10 It is when a person walks at night that they stumble, for
they have no light. 11 After he had said this, he went on to tell
them, "Our friend Lazarus has fallen asleep; but I am going
there to wake him up." 12 His disciples replied, "Lord, if he
sleeps, he will get better." 13 Jesus had been speaking of his
death, but his disciples thought he meant natural sleep. 14 So
then he told them plainly, "Lazarus is dead, 15 and for your
sake I am glad I was not there, so that you may believe. But let
us go to him. 16 Then Thomas (also known as Didymus) said to
the rest of the disciples, "Let us also go, that we may die with
him."
John 11: 7- 16 (NIV)

Possibly from the mind of Thomas…
First, we learn Lazarus is sick, yet you decide to stay here two
more days instead of going to check on him (the one you love).
Then you say we are going back, we remind you of the danger,
and you start talking about walking in daylight and night.
Finally, you say Lazarus is sleep, but dead, and you are going to
"wake him up". Enough already, let's just go back and get this
over with because I am confused. I've seen you do great things,
but I'm not sure about this one.

16 Then Thomas (also known as Didymus) said to the rest of the
disciples, "Let us also go, that we may die with him."

Have you ever had a Thomas moment or do you have Thomas moments?

I can admit I have them. Why? Following Jesus has the ability to shake our faith. His love takes us places we don't want to go and speaks words we don't always understand. His actions are confusing at times and if we are not careful, we could come away wondering if it's love or lunacy. Our finite minds are not equipped to handle the depths of His ways, so what we don't understand, we disregard or label as crazy. Faith won't let us stay there….

Our faith and trust in God, is the firm foundation under everything that makes life worth living. It's our handle on what we can't see. Hebrews 1: 11 (MSG)

So, we go…sometimes "Thomas-like", sometimes like the man who said, "I believe, but help my unbelief", but we go because it's better with Him than without Him.

Freedom

> *43 When he had said this, Jesus called in a loud voice,*
> *"Lazarus, come out!" 44 The dead man came out, his hands and*
> *feet wrapped with strips of linen, and a cloth around his face.*
> *Jesus said to them, "Take off the grave clothes and let him go."*
> *John 11: 43-44 (NIV)*

Lazarus was not the only one bound. When he walked out from the tomb, he and others were in need of grave clothing removal. The difference was Lazarus had been in a tomb, but others had been walking daily, wrapped in some form of grave clothing. There's an array of emotional challenges throughout this story, just as our life story is filled with things that would leave us bound and dead. Life's trials attack our faith, love, power, soundness of mind, and joy in the Lord.

God's glory can loosen us from those things that threaten to kill us with every struggle.
Jesus' love can free us from (see John 11 for verses below):
fear (verse 8)
confusion (verses 11-14)
frustration (verse 16)
anger (verse 20)
pain (verses 21-27)
doubt (verse 37)
disbelief (verses 39-40)

Are you in need of Grave Clothing Removal?

New creations

44 The dead man came out, his hands and feet bound with strips of cloth, and his face wrapped in a cloth. Jesus said to them, "Unbind him, and let him go."
John 11: 44 (NRSV)

Then he showed me the high priest Joshua standing before the angel of the Lord, and Satan standing at his right hand to accuse him. 2 And the Lord said to Satan, "The Lord rebuke you, O Satan! The Lord who has chosen Jerusalem rebuke you! Is not this man a brand plucked from the fire?" 3 Now Joshua was dressed with filthy clothes as he stood before the angel. 4 The angel said to those who were standing before him, "Take off his filthy clothes." And to him he said, "See, I have taken your guilt away from you, and I will clothe you with festal apparel." 5 And I said, "Let them put a clean turban on his head." So they put a clean turban on his head and clothed him with the apparel; and the angel of the Lord was standing by.
Zechariah 3: 1-5 (NRSV)

Great news for the believer!
Regardless of how the enemy tries to convince us otherwise; we do not have to be bound by grave clothes, nor walk around in filthy garments. By the word of God, we are loosed from the "death" we've been wrapped in and the guilt of the filth that has clothed us. The enemy stands to accuse, but Jesus rebukes him on every account and orders up new apparel designed for a joyous occasion. The occasion is a Freedom Festival! Freedom from guilt, shame, rejection, addiction, depression…anything that sets itself up against the love God has for us.

What does this new clothing look like?

Since God chose you to be the holy people he loves, you must clothe yourselves with tenderhearted mercy, kindness, humility, gentleness, and patience. 13 Make allowance for each other's faults, and forgive anyone who offends you. Remember, the Lord forgave you, so you must forgive others. Above all, clothe yourselves with love, which binds us all together in perfect harmony. 15 And let the peace that comes from Christ rule in your hearts. For as members of one body you are called to live in peace. And always be thankful.
Colossians 3: 12-15

Power

Overpowered!

Judas and the tough guys came to arrest Jesus. They came carrying their torches, lanterns, weapons, and hatred, but when Jesus identified himself as, "I AM he", something happened. What caused their change of position from intimidators to intimidated?

John 10: 17-18 (NIV)
17 The reason my Father loves me is that I lay down my life—only to take it up again. 18 No one takes it from me, but I lay it down of my own accord. I have authority to lay it down and authority to take it up again. This command I received from my Father."

Worldly weapons are no match for the power of God!

He sees

31 When the Lord saw that Leah was unloved, he opened her womb…
Genesis 29: 31-35 (CEB)

He sees…
Leah was unloved by her earthly father and husband.
She was the older and less attractive of the two sisters. In fact, Rachel is described as being lovely in form and beautiful, while Leah is described as being older with weak eyes. Her father used her to deceive Jacob to get free labor and marry off two daughters. As a result, Jacob did not love her as much as he loved Rachel. Leah was unloved.

He sees and He opens…
Leah was loved by her Heavenly Father.
She may not have looked like much to man, but to God she was fearfully and wonderfully made, a chosen vessel. God saw she was "unloved" by man and "He opened her womb…" The opening of her womb blessed her with one of the greatest gifts we have, the ability to give birth. To give birth is to bear (a child) or initiate/launch (an idea). God has given us all the ability to produce. Although we may be unloved by the world, the Lord loves us and opens opportunities for us to deliver. God desires to use us to bring something into existence, a gift we ought not to take lightly.

Misunderstanding our blessings

When the Lord saw that Leah was unloved, he opened her womb; but Rachel was unable to have children. 32 Leah became pregnant and gave birth to a son. She named him Reuben because she said, "The Lord saw my harsh treatment, and now my husband will love me." 33 She became pregnant again and gave birth to a son. She said, "The Lord heard that I was unloved, so he gave me this son too," and she named him Simeon. 34 She became pregnant again and gave birth to a son. She said, "Now, this time my husband will embrace me, since I have given birth to three sons for him." So she named him Levi. 35 She became pregnant again and gave birth to a son. She said, "This time I will praise the Lord." So she named him Judah. Then she stopped bearing children.
Genesis 29: 31-35 (CEB)

A misunderstanding of our abilities...our blessings...

Were you given the ability to sing for applause?
Were you given the ability to do mathematics to cheat?
Were you given the ability to supervise to humiliate?

Leah was given an open womb to give birth, but she misunderstood the purpose of her ability. With each birth, she looked for elevation and man's love. She was disappointed until she understood what to do with her blessings. She teaches us that we must stop producing for the glory of self and man. We need to develop a "This time..." attitude, every time. Then when we learn to praise God, we will have peace that goes beyond all understanding (even our own). At this point we will be able to say with confidence in faith, "I will praise God".

Judgmental Thoughts

39 When the Pharisee who had invited him saw this, he said to himself, "If this man were a prophet, he would know what kind of woman is touching him. She's a sinner!" 40 Then Jesus answered his thoughts.
Luke 7: 39-40, 44-46, (NLT)

Simon's thoughts, on the surface, appear to judge the woman, "She's a sinner!" But, his intent is to question Jesus. Unfortunately, it is easy to sit back and judge who and what we see. We observe, then take our limited information (we rarely know the entire story), mix in our self-righteousness with a dash of our own shortcomings and form sanctimonious conclusions.
"What's the difference? They can't hear what I'm thinking, anyway."
They can't, but Jesus can and He is offended. satan stands to accuse us regularly and Jesus speaks on our behalf for every accusation.
Who are we to judge? For every sin we point out in others, we have at least three of our own.

44 Then he turned to the woman and said to Simon, "Look at this woman kneeling here. When I entered your home, you didn't offer me water to wash the dust from my feet, but she has washed them with her tears and wiped them with her hair. 45 You didn't greet me with a kiss, but from the time I first came in, she has not stopped kissing my feet. 46 You neglected the courtesy of olive oil to anoint my head, but she has anointed my feet with rare perfume.

Jesus noted three opportunities Simon had to worship Him, but because he was busy thinking, he missed the chance to worship

in spirit and in truth. Simon's mind was more interested in judgment and gossip.
It's not enough to watch what we say; we must guard our minds/thoughts, too.

…we take every thought captive and make it obey Christ.
2 Corinthians 10: 5

Loving our neighbors

45 And the leper's clothes shall be rent, and the hair of his head shall hang loose, and he shall cover his upper lip and cry, Unclean, unclean! 46 He shall remain unclean as long as the disease is in him; he is unclean; he shall live alone [and] his dwelling shall be outside the camp.
Leviticus 13: 45-46 (AMP)

Who lives outside the camp?
A leper is a person having leprosy (skin disease) OR someone rejected by and considered an outcast by society. Who lives outside your camp, the lepers of your world? My lepers and your lepers may or may not be the same, so consider the following questions.

Who is not "clean" enough to live in your camp?
Who do you not touch…physically (keep your distance), mentally (you rarely give them any thought), spiritually (they are too far gone to pray for), or emotionally (look the other way)?
Who have you allowed society to deem an outcast, thereby justifying their mistreatment?

Do you recognize your lepers (sometimes we don't)? I do and I am convicted by my thoughts and behavior. I recently read a book about getting to know Jesus and one chapter discussed His compassion. The author used the example of Jesus healing the leper by touching him. The author raised the point that Jesus did not have to touch him in order to heal him. He chose to touch the untouchable. Something about the truth of what Jesus did hit me like a ton of bricks! My initial thoughts were of the magnitude of His compassion, followed by the realization of the world's lack of compassion (me included). I thought of those who live "outside" our camps…How dare we avoid, give no thought to, not pray for, and ignore our brothers and sisters and claim to love Jesus.

A man with leprosy came and knelt in front of Jesus, begging to be healed. "If you are willing, you can heal me and make me clean," he said. 41 Moved with compassion, Jesus reached out and touched him. "I am willing," he said. "Be healed!" 42 Instantly the leprosy disappeared, and the man was healed.
Mark 1: 40-42

Does our love for Jesus extend outside our camps?

Righteousness

4 Everyone who makes a practice of sinning also practices lawlessness; sin is lawlessness. 5 You know that he appeared in order to take away sins, and in him there is no sin. 6 No one who abides in him keeps on sinning; no one who keeps on sinning has either seen him or known him. 7 Little children, let no one deceive you. Whoever practices righteousness is righteous, as he is righteous. 8 Whoever makes a practice of sinning is of the devil, for the devil has been sinning from the beginning. The reason the Son of God appeared was to destroy the works of the devil.
1 John 3: 4-8 (ESV)

Practice makes perfect! Isn't that what parents, coaches, and teachers love to promote? If you want to get good at something, practice.

What is it about practice that can make you better? Practice is planned (you know you are going to do it), intentional (you have a reason for doing it), focused (your mind is stayed on what you are practicing), and done regularly (you do it frequently).

So, what do you practice…righteousness or sin?

I considered all my practices that could be considered righteous…Bible study, encouraging others, looking out for widows and orphans, etc. I felt pretty righteous until God caused me to consider some of my other "practices". For example, being quick to judge, unloving, unforgiving, doubtful, etc…

It's not so simple, I try to practice righteousness, but for every righteous act there's a sin or two keeping me from what I desire most, God's glory.

So, what gives? What practice will bring God glory?

No one who abides in him keeps on sinning 1 John 3: 6
This righteousness is given through faith in Jesus Christ to all who
believe... Romans 3: 22a

If practice is planned, intentional, focused, and done regularly,
then through faith, practice abiding in Him. He is the vine; we
are the branches and apart from Him we can do nothing, not
even "practice" righteousness.

"They"

And immediately there was in their synagogue a man with an unclean spirit. And he cried out, 24 "What have you to do with us, Jesus of Nazareth? Have you come to destroy us? I know who you are—the Holy One of God."
Mark 1: 23-24 (ESV)

We go to church regularly. We know who Jesus is, we talk to Him, know His power and authority, but so do "they".

"They" enter our places of worship and talk to Jesus. "They" know who He is, His power and His authority. The unclean spirit knew who Jesus was, talked to Him, asked a question, then identified Him as the Holy One of God. Believers know who Jesus is, talk to Him, ask questions, and declare Him holy. One might wonder, what's the difference…

We confess with our mouths and believe in our hearts that Jesus is Lord; the enemy speaks with his mouth and believes in his heart that he, himself, is lord. (John 10: 10, 1 John 3: 10, Romans 10: 9)

Burdens

Heaviness in the heart of man maketh it stoop...
Proverbs 12: 25 (KJV)

Do not be wise in your own eyes; fear the Lord and shun evil.
8This will bring health to your body and nourishment to your
bones.
Proverbs 3: 7-8 (NIV)

Many times our spiritual ailments show up physically.

We carry what is too heavy for us. We carry it, but not without
it being a strain on our back, neck, and shoulders. We may find
ourselves stooping to compensate for the load, in turn causing
deformities and pain. The pain affects the body and mind as we
suffer needlessly; bearing weight we are not strong enough to
lift. Why do we foolishly carry what is too heavy for us? We
have many excuses for being wise in our own eyes..."It's not
too heavy; I can handle it. There's no one else to carry it. I
don't want any help."

I was referring to what we physically carry, but what about the
loads we bear that can't be seen? They have the ability to cause
us strain, wear, and tear. We have the same foolish excuses for
carrying guilt, unforgiveness, labels, and fear (to name a few).

Turmoil on the inside comes out one way or another.

Coming to yourself

...and there he wasted his fortune in reckless and loose [from restraint] living. 14 And when he had spent all he had, a mighty famine came upon that country, and he began to fall behind and be in want. 15 So he went and forced (glued) himself upon one of the citizens of that country, who sent him into his fields to feed hogs. 16 And he would gladly have fed on and filled his belly with the carob pods that the hogs were eating, but [they could not satisfy his hunger and] nobody gave him anything [better]. 17 Then when he came to himself...
Luke 15: 13-17 (AMP)

Do you remember when you came to yourself?

There comes a point in our lives when we realize we have been wasting our time and gifts. We've been living recklessly, feeding on what is not satisfying and living in low places. We are all the Prodigal Son. Some conveniently don't identify with the story because they didn't live "recklessly", partying was not their "thing". Perhaps you were not a wild child, but you may have been a gossiper. Maybe you were not promiscuous, but you may have acted on your anger. Let's just say you didn't have any addictions, but you were deep in debt. Reckless living is living without honoring God and looking for the world to satisfy a need that only the Lord can. So, come on in, take a seat, and join the rest of us who squandered our "resources".

The moment of coming to yourself is the moment you realize you could and should be living better. It is a good practice to reflect upon your hog feeding days and give praise for God's faithfulness.

Roles we play

20 "So he returned home to his father. And while he was still a long way off, his father saw him coming. Filled with love and compassion, he ran to his son, embraced him, and kissed him. 21 His son said to him, 'Father, I have sinned against both heaven and you, and I am no longer worthy of being called your son.' 22 "But his father said to the servants, 'Quick! Bring the finest robe in the house and put it on him. Get a ring for his finger and sandals for his feet. 23 And kill the calf we have been fattening. We must celebrate with a feast, 24 for this son of mine was dead and has now returned to life. He was lost, but now he is found.' So the party began.
Luke 15: 20-32 (NLT)

So much to celebrate…the son recognizes his need for the father, the father sees him before he arrives and lovingly greets him, the son confesses his unworthiness, the father throws a party because his son has come back to life!! So much to celebrate, unless you are the older brother.

25 "Meanwhile, the older son was in the fields working. When he returned home, he heard music and dancing in the house, 26 and he asked one of the servants what was going on. 27 'Your brother is back,' he was told, 'and your father has killed the fattened calf. We are celebrating because of his safe return.' 28 "The older brother was angry and wouldn't go in.

One of the things I love about God is that He will reveal who we really are and expose the various roles we play (as in present tense and continuing). We love the Prodigal Son when we acknowledge that we have strayed and been welcomed back, but tend to be hard on the older brother until we admit we have been him, too. In fact, I can say I was the "older brother" before the Prodigal Son. I looked around and wondered why the unrighteous seemed to have what I wanted. I felt as though I was doing the right things, yet they were receiving MY blessing!

His father came out and begged him, 29 but he replied, 'All these years I've slaved for you and never once refused to do a single thing you told me to. And in all that time you never gave me even one young goat for a feast with my friends. 30 Yet when this son of yours comes back after squandering your money on prostitutes, you celebrate by killing the fattened calf!' 31 "His father said to him, 'Look, dear son, you have always stayed by me, and everything I have is yours. 32 We had to celebrate this happy day. For your brother was dead and has come back to life! He was lost, but now he is found!'"

The point is not which came first, the Prodigal Son or the Older Brother. The point is we waver between the two until we stop looking at what our brothers are doing and realize God is not partial. We cannot bribe Him with our self-righteousness. What we often miss and what I am so very thankful for is that the Father meets both brothers where they are…the Prodigal Son in his unrighteousness and the Pharisee (I mean older brother) in his self-righteousness.

Let the party begin!

Be alert

Be alert, be on watch!
Your enemy, the Devil, roams around like a roaring lion,
looking for someone to devour.
1 Peter 5: 8 (GNT)

The word "be" is defined in a few ways, such as, "to exist or live, occupy a place or position, or to continue (or remain as before)".

Peter strongly urges us to exist, live, occupy a position of, and continue in spiritual alertness and watchfulness. Our enemy, the devil, continually roams the earth looking to destroy us. Therefore, we must occupy a place of cautiousness against our enemy where we have our full armor on, our sword sharpened and ready for battle, our minds stayed on God, where we are walking in peace and wrapped in truth, our faith is intact, and we know Christ is our righteousness.

Being aware and on the lookout for the enemy will not deter his attacks, but it will remind him that our God fights for us and he (the devil) has already been defeated!

An encouraging word

…but an encouraging word makes it glad.
Proverbs 12: 25 (AMP)

Be that person!
Take time today to resist the temptation to grumble and
complain about your life, aches, and pains. Trade your
heaviness, at least once today, for an encouraging word to
another person. We have relationships where we get too
comfortable sharing our load (dumping) and never take a
moment to share a positive word with our brothers and sisters.
 I was privileged to know a man that always had a word of hope
even when he could've complained. He had a way of making
you think he had been waiting all day to see you. He would light
up, grab your hand or hug you and say something as lovely as,
"Good morning!" It was lovely because those two simple
words were laced with the love of God and he really meant
GOOD morning.

Be that person; you can't go wrong. It won't take anything
away from you to set yourself aside and makes someone else's
heart glad. It might even remove some of your own heaviness.

Clean heart / sin

Care for the flock that God has entrusted to you.
Watch over it willingly, not grudgingly—
not for what you will get out of it, but because you are eager
to serve God.
3 Don't lord it over the people assigned to your care, but lead
them by your own good example.
1 Peter 5: 2-3 (NLT)

How often do we grudgingly carry out our responsibilities, seek
what we can get out of the "deal", and/or mismanage those
under our care?

I am convicted as I reflect on the many times I have lost sight of
the fact the Lord has ENTRUSTED His "flock" to me. Peter's
words serve as a reminder as I prepare for work. The place I
report to…who I work with…and the tasks I must complete,
belong to Him. He is entrusting me to care for it/them with a
willingness and eagerness that reflects Him. Each day presents
us with the opportunity to be an imitator of God.
May the Lord forgive my unrighteousness and create in me a
clean heart, renewed and ready to serve His will.

Clean heart / sin

5 *We demolish arguments and every pretension that sets itself
up against the knowledge of God, and we take captive every
thought to make it obedient to Christ.*
2 Corinthians 10: 5 (NIV)

I must admit when God revealed I had a pride problem, my first
reaction was, "I object!"
Pride is tricky like that…

I began to search scripture for "pride". I found words like
haughty, lofty, lifted eyes, stubborn, and arrogance. Not only
did I find those words in common, but pride was connected to
the heart/mind and mouth. Like I said, pride is tricky. Not
every pride-filled person is "puffed up" on the outside, some of
us are puffed up on the inside. It's what we meditate
on…what's inside our hearts and minds. It's our own private
battle that left unchecked, will come busting out.

God has shown me my issue(s) lie in two statements I meditate
on too often…
I'm not doing (fill in the blank).
I'm not dealing with (insert name) or a given situation.
I feel it in my heart, then speak it with my mouth. Every time I
meditate on and speak those statements, I negate my mission.
 Those words/thoughts set themselves up against the
knowledge of God. The Word tells us to make every thought
obedient to Christ, not to self. The question becomes, "Who
am I serving? Self or God?" My "I'm not…" statements serve
me.

Dear Lord, Let the words of my mouth, and the meditation of my heart, be acceptable in thy sight. O Lord, my strength, and my redeemer, strengthen me to make every thought, from the enemy and the inner me, obedient to you, in Jesus name.

Heart / sin

Create in me a new, clean heart, O God, filled with clean
thoughts and right desires.
Psalm 51: 10 (TLB)

I lean into, trust, and depend on God to perform this spiritual
heart surgery. The procedure...the cutting away is painful and
reveals ugly truths. A new and clean heart cannot be completed
without exposing the dirt, crud, and hardness of the existing
heart. The enemy shows up for the surgery and stands on the
side lines in order to mock the procedure. he heckles while
God prunes and cuts and removes. his mission is to take the
ugliness and magnify it until you forget it's been cut away...no
longer a part of you.

Then their eyes were opened, and they both realized that they were
naked. They sewed fig leaves together and made clothes for themselves.
Genesis 3: 7 (GW)

The enemy condemns and moves on.

In the cool of the evening, the man and his wife heard the Lord God
walking around in the garden. So they hid from the Lord God among
the trees in the garden. 9 The Lord God called to the man and asked
him, "Where are you?" 10 He answered, "I heard you in the garden. I was
afraid because I was naked, so I hid." 11 God asked, "Who told you that
you were naked? Did you eat fruit from the tree I commanded you not to
eat from?"

21 The Lord God made clothes from animal skins for the man and his
wife and dressed them. Genesis 3: 8-11, 21 (GW)

God reveals…exposes (convicts), then covers, never leaves, nor forsakes.

God wants to know where we are, not because He is unaware, but so we can face our "low-cation". Once exposed, we are free to invite Him to do a make-over or should we say a make-better!

Fools

"Stay away from a fool, because you will not receive knowledge from his lips."
Proverbs 14

BEWARE:
Attributes of a fool…
A fool tears down (v. 1)
A fool talks and talks - indiscriminately (v. 3, 23)
A fool bears false witness - lies on others (v. 5, 25)
A fool treats righteousness with scorn or contempt (v. 6, 9)
A fool lacks knowledge (v. 7)
A fool lacks good judgment (v. 8, 18, 24)
A fool is simple-minded (v. 15, 18)
A fool is hotheaded, reckless and quick-tempered (v. 16, 17, 29)
A fool is crafty (devious intentions) (v. 17, 22)
A fool is a shameful servant (v. 35)

God gives us direction so that we can avoid the fools around us and within us!

Hardships

"We must go through many hardships to enter the kingdom of God," they said.
Acts 14: 22b

The Book of Acts illustrates the highs and lows of ministry. The apostles went from conversions to opposition, from preaching and reaching to jealousy and stoning, from healings to beatings and imprisonment, from fellowship to the parting of ways with ministry partners, from saving souls through Christ to accusations and misunderstandings.

Through many hardships they continued to move, preach the good news, be bold in Jesus Christ, encourage and strengthen each other, and obey (knowing when to stay and when to move).

Spiritually blind

Blind (in darkness), groping, and seeking for someone to take our hand…
Acts 13:11 AMP

The amplified version paints a perfect picture of what it feels like to be caught in sin, know it or not.

The parallels between Saul's and Elymas' blindness are interesting. Both were spiritually blind and made physically blind as a vehicle to salvation. God had plans for Saul (Acts 9:15); he was God's chosen instrument. But Elymas' blindness led Sergius Paulus, the proconsul, to salvation. Sergius Paulus became a believer after watching and hearing the Holy Spirit's anointing on Saul and Barnabas.

The use of the word "intelligent" to describe Sergius Paulus is another similarity in the story of blindness leading to "sight". The Amplified Bible describes him as "an intelligent and sensible man of sound understanding". Saul was also known for his intelligence, but intelligence does not always lend itself to wisdom. Wisdom comes from God and sometimes our intelligence blocks true wisdom, knowledge, and understanding.

From this point on, there is no more use of the name Saul in the book of Acts. Paul and Sergius Paulus became new creatures in Jesus Christ; they received new identities.

Move

14 But they [themselves] came on from Perga and arrived at Antioch in Pisidia. And on the Sabbath day they went into the synagogue there and sat down.15 After the reading of the Law and the Prophets, the leaders [of the worship] of the synagogue sent to them saying, Brethren, if you have any word of exhortation or consolation or encouragement for the people, say it. 16 So Paul arose, and motioning with his hand said, Men of Israel and you who reverence and fear God, listen! Acts 13: 14-16, 44-52

44 The next Sabbath almost the entire city gathered together to hear the Word of God [concerning the attainment through Christ of salvation in the kingdom of God].45 But when the Jews saw the crowds, filled with envy and jealousy they contradicted what was said by Paul and talked abusively [reviling and slandering him].46 And Paul and Barnabas spoke out plainly and boldly, saying, It was necessary that God's message [concerning salvation through Christ] should be spoken to you first. But since you thrust it from you, you pass this judgment on yourselves that you are unworthy of eternal life and out of your own mouth you will be judged. [Now] behold, we turn to the Gentiles (the heathen).47 For so the Lord has charged us, saying, I have set you to be a light for the Gentiles (the heathen), that you may bring [eternal] salvation to the uttermost parts of the earth.48 And when the Gentiles heard this, they rejoiced and glorified (praised and gave thanks for) the Word of God; and as many as were destined (appointed and ordained) to eternal life believed (adhered to, trusted in, and relied on Jesus as the Christ and their Savior).49 And so the Word of the Lord [concerning eternal salvation through Christ] scattered and spread throughout the whole region.

50 But the Jews stirred up the devout women of high rank and the outstanding men of the town, and instigated persecution against Paul and Barnabas and drove them out of their boundaries.

51 But [the apostles] shook off the dust from their feet against them and went to Iconium.

52 And the disciples were continually filled [throughout their souls] with joy and the Holy Spirit.

God blessed Paul and Barnabas to spread the word and move on.

Paul preached about God's salvation from Abraham to Jesus. The people invited them back for the next Sabbath; they wanted more of the word! News spread about their anointing to preach the word and "almost the whole city gathered to hear the word of the Lord". Jealousy reared its ugly head, one thing led to another; Paul and Barnabas were expelled from that region. The Jews were caught up in the world and the people were caught up in the "word". They gathered, not for Paul and Barnabas, but for the word of God. There are some people who do not have a heart for the message you share and it doesn't matter what you do or how you do it; they will always find fault. We have to know when to shake the dust off our feet and move on.

The good part about God-ordained moving on is that there is no need for hard feelings when you have fulfilled your assignment. They moved on with no remorse, but with joy and the Holy Spirit. The *great* part about God-driven moving on…God receives the glory. Verse 49 reads, "The word of the Lord spread through the whole region."

If you have finished the assignment God has given you, shake the dust off and head for the next chapter.

Know Jesus for yourself

> *"I command you by the Jesus preached by Paul!"* The Message
> *"I command you in the name of Jesus, whom Paul preaches,..."* NLT
> *"In the name of Jesus, whom Paul preaches,..."* NIV
> *Acts 19: 13*

The importance of knowing Jesus for ourselves...
He shouldn't be the Jesus of our mother, father, or best friend;
He should be our Jesus. We should be in such intimate
relationship with Him that we claim Him as our own. The Sons
of Sceva help us to see the importance of NOT talking about
and claiming what we don't know for ourselves!

Be Quiet

14 But just as Paul started to make his defense, Gallio turned to Paul's accusers and said, "Listen, you Jews, if this were a case involving some wrongdoing or a serious crime, I would have a reason to accept your case. 15 But since it is merely a question of words and names and your Jewish law, take care of it yourselves. I refuse to judge such matters." 16 And he threw them out of the courtroom.
Acts 18: 14-16

Paul was passionate; he lived and died to preach the good news of Jesus Christ. He was told from the start he would suffer greatly and he did, but it did not discourage him. Paul spoke boldly with the anointing of the Holy Spirit. He was an intelligent, articulate and engaging speaker. His preaching drew emotion from the people; good and bad. Paul's routine was to go to the synagogue and "reason" with the Jews and Greeks. I can only imagine the tension as they debated. Yet, in Acts 18:14, Paul begins to defend himself and is cut off by Gallio, the proconsul.

Regardless of how verbally and oratorically gifted we are, there is a time to be quiet. For whatever reason, Paul did not need to speak. God put someone else in place to do the talking. I find this helpful for times I feel misunderstood and want to defend myself. I don't always have to speak.

Leadership

18 When they arrived he declared, "You know that from the day I set foot in the province of Asia until now 19 I have done the Lord's work humbly and with many tears. I have endured the trials that came to me from the plots of the Jews. 20 I never shrank back from telling you what you needed to hear, either publicly or in your homes. 21 I have had one message for Jews and Greeks alike—the necessity of repenting from sin and turning to God, and of having faith in our Lord Jesus.

22 "And now I am bound by the Spirit to go to Jerusalem. I don't know what awaits me, 23 except that the Holy Spirit tells me in city after city that jail and suffering lie ahead. 24 But my life is worth nothing to me unless I use it for finishing the work assigned me by the Lord Jesus—the work of telling others the Good News about the wonderful grace of God.

25 "And now I know that none of you to whom I have preached the Kingdom will ever see me again. 26 I declare today that I have been faithful. If anyone suffers eternal death, it's not my fault, 27 for I didn't shrink from declaring all that God wants you to know. 28 "So guard yourselves and God's people. Feed and shepherd God's flock—his church, purchased with his own blood—over which the Holy Spirit has appointed you as elders. 29 I know that false teachers, like vicious wolves, will come in among you after I leave, not sparing the flock. 30 Even some men from your own group will rise up and distort the truth in order to draw a following. 31 Watch out! Remember the three years I was with you—my constant watch and care over you night and day, and my many tears for you. 32 "And now I entrust you to God and the message of his grace that is able to build you up and give you an inheritance with all those he has set apart for himself.

Acts 20: 18-32

One of the things I love about Paul is his leadership. He was a great leader, one of sound integrity. Paul's first love was the Lord, then the people. He preached the salvation of Jesus Christ tirelessly because he was chosen to. Often times, we associate "leadership" with a title, but we are called to lead in whatever position we find ourselves in. We must lead where we are. A few leadership points from Paul:

- A good leader knows he/she will not be in that specific appointed place of leadership forever. (Acts 20:25)
- A good leader wants the mission to be carried out, even in their absence; therefore, he/she prepares and equips others to move forward. (Acts 20: 28-35)
- A good leader sees the big picture and understands it is greater than them. (Acts 23: 11)
- A good leader knows what needs to be shared and what does not. (Acts 23: 11)

One thing we tend to overlook about good leaders is their ability to follow. I am convinced that Paul's leadership was directly connected to his ability to follow.

Although he was aware of the hardships and imprisonments ahead, he was obedient to God's assignment. Those who loved him pleaded with him not to go to Jerusalem, yet he went. Twice it was stated that Paul could have been set free, but he chose God's will. Just as we watch our leaders, God watches our following.

Representatives

Be wise in the way you act toward outsiders; make the most of every opportunity. Let your conversation be always full of grace, seasoned with salt, so that you may know how to answer everyone.
Colossians 4: 5-6 (NIV)

Every day provides another opportunity to be a witness for God. Our disposition is the first thing noticed by others. In other words, if I am unapproachable, I may not get a chance to witness. When was the last time you approached an unapproachable person? I don't make a habit of it. If I can find a store representative with a more positive attitude, guess who I am going to for assistance…We are God's representatives.

Once there is an opening, what do "outsiders" hear? If we are complaining and gossiping, what sets us apart? Our conversation should be positively inviting. I like 'seasoned with salt' because salt is used as a preservative. To preserve is to keep safe from harm or injury; protect or spare, to keep up; maintain. People should feel safe with us; not on the offense. When a safe environment has been created, people feel comfortable asking what sets us apart or where we get our "seasoning" from.

Sadly, and too often lately, I've missed opportunities to minister because I've been focused on the inconveniences around me. It shows on my face even when I don't say a word. Colossians 4: 5-6 reminds me to pray, for not only the words of my words, but also my countenance to be pleasing and acceptable to God. I am God's representative. We are God's representatives.

Consumed

My soul is consumed with longing for your laws at all times.
Psalm 119: 20 (NIV)

What do you want to receive? What do you buy? Who do you desire to have?
Are the answers connected to God…a greater desire for His word…a closer relationship with Him?

What kind of person is consumed with longing for God?
Is it the pastor who has been "assigned" to ponder the wonders of God? Is it the elderly person? Or is it the one with no social life so they become consumed with God? In other words, who would choose to be consumed with longing for God when there are so many other things and people to desire?

After reflecting over my own life, I have discovered God is it.
 I've longed for people and things only to be disappointed. God is faithful; He is the same yesterday, today, and forever. He accepts me as I am, but leaves room for growth. He is always true to His word, no false advertisements.

So, now is the time to be filled up, wrapped up and tied up in God!

A light for my path...

Your word is a lamp to guide my feet and a light for my path. (NLT)
Psalm 119: 105

By your words I can see where I'm going; they throw a beam of light on my dark path. (MSG)

One summer evening while on vacation, my husband and I decided to take an evening stroll, not realizing how dark it would become. We could barely see in front of us so we used the flashlight from our cell phones to make sure we didn't trip over branches, uneven sidewalks, or anything else that might cause us to fall. We were walking in a residential area with enough light for us to see the path in front of us, but no bright city lights illuminating our way. So, we had a lamp for our feet and a light for our path. We didn't necessarily see our destination, but we were able to move along with enough light to keep us afoot until we arrived. We had enough light to know we were moving in the right direction.

We have no idea what a new year will bring, but God's word will provide the guidance we need.

To Contact the author

AmAradia

likeatreeplanted2016@gmail.com

Follow me on Twitter and Instagram
@LikeTreePlanted

Check out my blogs at
butterfliesandothertransformations.blogspot.com
stayrootedlikeatree.blogspot.com